SA~~FELY~~
HOME

OTHER BOOKS FROM VISION FORUM

Poems for Patriarchs

Missionary Patriarch

How God Wants Us to Worship Him

Home-Making

Mother

The Bible Lessons of John Quincy Adams for His Son

The Letters and Lessons of Teddy Roosevelt for His Son

The Sinking of the Titanic

Of Plymouth Plantation

The Elsie Dinsmore Series

Cabin on the Prairie

Cabin in the Northwoods

Pollard's Child's History of America

Sergeant York and the Great War

The Life and Campaigns of Stonewall Jackson

The Boys' Guide to the
Historical Adventures of G.A. Henty

SAFELY HOME

TOM ELDREDGE
Foreword by Doug Phillips

Then answered Jesus and said unto them,
Verily, verily, I say unto you, The Son can do
nothing of himself, but what he seeth the
Father do: for what things soever he doeth,
these also doeth the Son likewise.
For the Father loveth the Son, and sheweth
him all things that himself doeth.
John 5:19–20

THE VISION FORUM, INC.
San Antonio, Texas

To my brothers:
Bob, John, and Curt

CONTENTS

Foreword ix

Acknowledgments xiii

Introduction 1

1. Education and Relationships 3

2. Leaving Home: The Decline of the Family 5

3. Greek Education and the Gymnasium 13

4. The Decline of Hebrew Education .25

5. The Development of the American Public School 43

6. Developing a Biblical Philosophy of Education 55

7. A Helping Hand Toward Home 69

8. Steps in Rebuilding 83

9. A Safe Course Lies Ahead 95

Endnotes 105

Bibliography 109

Foreword

The American Church spent the better part of the twentieth century living with the implications of the isms of the nineteenth. The "revivalism" of Finney and others became the intellectual predecessor to the technique-driven, program-based church. The evolutionism of the nineteenth century gave us a sociological approach to worship which demanded age segregation. The egalitarianism of the post-Civil War era taught us to view the local church as a connection of completely independent individuals, instead of as members of families, of covenanting communities, and as heirs to a patriarchal legacy. Likewise, the feminism of the post-industrial revolution, driven in part by the rise in absentee fathers, turned the church into a matriarchal society with women as the primary communicators of spiritual truths to the next generation.

By the twentieth century, the combined effect of these noxious, anti-familistic isms, had finally taken its toll on the local church, transforming many into baby sitting operations, psychological rehab centers, and size-driven experiments in mass marketing—anything but the family-affirming community of saints required by Scripture.

But perhaps someday we will look back upon the early years of the twenty-first century as the turning point.

What happened?

After years of broken marriages, rebellious children, and misplaced priorities within the Church, some parents have begun to cry out to God. The cry has been answered by a Holy Spirit-driven desire on the part of fathers to turn their hearts to their children, by the rise of the home education movement with its emphasis on parent-directed Hebrew education, and with the wonderful rediscovery of historical and biblical roles for men and for women.

Even more importantly, many of these parents recognize that apart from their ability to intimately know Jesus Christ and to communicate the kind of obedience that He showed to the Father, that their best laid plans for family revival will fail.

Remarkably, many church shepherds are catching on to the fact that, despite a smorgasbord of programs, the majority of the children born to believing parents will reject the faith of their fathers and blend into an increasingly pagan society. They, too, grieve at the destruction of the family within their flocks, but they are at a loss for what to do.

The significance of the book in your hands is that it offers concrete, biblical solutions to the crisis of priorities between the church, the family, and the culture of our day. In this sense, the book is not only timely, it is historic, because it marks one of the first of what we hope will be many books which directly address the all-important need for revival and reformation between the family and the church—a revival which can occur when men reject "Greek" lifestyles, education programs, and business philosophies, in exchange for a distinctively "Hebrew" approach to family life and culture.

Here is great hope for fathers and mothers. Men need not fear. They need not live under the bondage of misplaced priorities, of wrong lifestyle choices, of family-segregating educational philosophies, or local churches driven by youth culture. Men (and women, too) can go safely home.

Thank you, Tom, for the courage to communicate what we so

desperately needed to hear, but few were willing to say. May God give a mighty vision to many, and may family reformation spread throughout the Church.

Doug Phillips
The Vision Forum, Inc.
San Antonio, Texas
March 2002

Acknowledgments

I f any blessing comes from this book, let the Lord Jesus Christ receive all the glory.

I have dedicated this book to my three brothers. Without their support, I could not have written it. We are commanded in the Scriptures to "love as brethren" (1 Peter 3:8). The relationships in the local church are defined for each of us by the relationships we know in our own families. Growing up and working together under the leadership of my oldest brother, Bob, has meant so much to me that I want to ensure that my children (nine, so far) will learn to appreciate how priceless the relationship between brothers and sisters can be if they will nurture it as young children. That is why home schooling means so much to me. Our children are learning much more than academic subjects in the home. They are learning at a young age that their brothers and sisters *are* their best friends. So, thank you, Bob, John, and Curt, for providing one of the driving forces for my life.

My thanks to all my friends who have let me talk their ears off as I tried out my thoughts on them. There is one thing I know: the Lord has used me to increase the patience of all my friends and acquaintances.

Many thanks to my wife, who tolerated the light shining in our bedroom night after night. My thanks also to that fine grammar teacher (also my wife) who struggled to teach me the proper placement of commas until she realized I was a hopeless cause. I was one student too many, and I am not as teachable as her others. Thank you Helen, Grace, Tommy, Daniel, David, Joel, Andrew, Carl, Susanne, and Benjamin for allowing me the time to see these exciting things in God's Word and for helping me see where I need to be discipled. You helped me know what to write. I hope every member of my family is glad that I wrote this book. I know they yearn for the day when I will be a better spiritual leader for our family. I hope writing this book will help (James 3:1).

My thanks go out to Pastor Allen Griffith, who helped me to see my independent spirit. I am obliged to Dr. James R. Truax, John W. Thompson, and Richard W. Sinclair, shepherds and teachers who helped me to understand the role of the local church in home schooling. I also thank Brother Clyde D. Gwin for sharing his concerns as a shepherd, for struggling through my rough drafts, and for pastoring me.

I will not forget Debra A. Marr's encouragement and how she generously donated her time to help get the early versions of this manuscript together before the deadline. My thanks to Ward and Ann Bartsch for their insights and encouragement. Bill Lechner, I appreciate your perseverance and your help in writing the most tender section in the book. It seemed as though until you came alongside to help, Satan would not allow me to break through and express the burdens I had in my heart for fathers. I am indebted to Mrs. Inge Cannon for her helpful suggestions. Inge, you have convinced me that I need to take a beginning grammar course, majoring in participial phrases and comma punctuation. I wish to acknowledge Bill Gothard and the folks at the Institute in Basic Life Principles. I do not know where my thoughts end and the things you have taught me begin—they so permeate my thinking. Thank you, Mrs. Robert Harkins, my mom, for your criticisms and for helping me see more of my blind spots. It has been said before that a mother is a man's best critic. Sometimes this is hard to receive, but I am reminded again of its truth.

I take full credit for any and all errors in this book. As much as each of these folks and others have tried to help it reach perfection, I have still managed to keep this book very human.

Finally, I owe a debt of gratitude to all of the home schoolers who have shared enough of their lives with me to convince me that working to help home schooling parents is a most worthwhile investment. Each of them has helped to turn the hearts of other fathers to their children (Malachi 4:6).

Introduction

I
t is a jungle out there for the new home schooler. New Age ideas and humanistic philosophies are thriving within the home school movement. Parents are following shepherds they do not know in search of direction. Thus far, churches have not been the ones who have led the Christian home schoolers. How long will this trend continue?

The primary goal of this book is to show why local churches should lead and support parent educators in their congregations. After defining and studying God's pattern for the education of children, it should be clear that there is no other institution that can fill the needs of Christian home schoolers. After reading this book, I pray the reader will also understand why local churches need the home schoolers as much as the home schoolers need the church.

An additional purpose for this book is to provide a much-needed historical review of the family in three ancient civilizations which have shaped western civilization, showing the relationship between the care of children's minds (education) and other indicators of a civilization's general health. For the skeptics (as I once was) I hope this study adequately explains why the ancient Hebrews turned from home schooling to professional educators and schools for the education of their children—and the results of that turn.

I believe there are many godly shepherds who have been struggling to help their congregations stay close to the Lord and who are now noticing what God is doing in the home schooling movement. I believe God is right now bringing an answer to their prayers through the home schoolers He is raising up. These shepherds have many sincere questions concerning home schooling. I hope this book provides the serious answers they deserve.

I have written this book out of a heart of concern and a growing excitement. God has surely been turning the hearts of fathers to their children, and we are beginning to see the fruit of this work in our own family and in our friends' families. Now we are beginning to see the home school movement make the other necessary turn, the turn back to the local church. It is my hope that this book will help my brothers and sisters in Christ make this last turn and arrive *safely home*.

CHAPTER ONE

Education and Relationships

The first conflict in recorded history was a battle over education. In His love for His creatures, God graciously revealed a vast body of knowledge to Adam. He clearly intended to share much more as He walked with Adam daily in the Garden. This relationship of the Creator to His creature formed the basis of an educational process that could be described as the first discipleship program.

For Adam and Eve the process was not fast enough. Why wait for God to reveal knowledge when you could simply eat some fruit and "have your eyes opened?" Adam took what seemed like a shortcut to knowledge—and he gave up the relationship he had with His God. Since then, Satan has never forgotten that man tends to sacrifice relationship for knowledge.

From our twentieth-century American perspective, it might be tempting to excuse Adam's decision as an experiment in efficiency. After all, Adam's responsibilities seem enormous to modern eyes. God expected him to have dominion over the whole animal kingdom. He must have been a busy man. How critical can we be of Adam?

We are so efficiency-minded today that we leave little time for things in life that take time—things like relationships, discipling our children, and helping others. People have always had twenty-four hours in a day, and today we have more timesaving devices than any generation before us. One would think we would have *more* time for the relationships God desires for the family and the church. Instead, Satan sees that we have less. It is as though a thief has stolen our time and our relationships. In fact, he has.

We are a "nation at risk" today—but not because we do not place a high priority on the education of children. Our failure in the educational world exists because we have failed to understand the importance of relationships: relationships with God, relationships in the family, and relationships within the local church.

It is time for Christian leaders to reexamine the Word of God to discover what He has revealed regarding the education and training of children. We can no longer continue to adopt what we have learned about efficiency in our factories to the training of our children. We have developed a thirteen-year program run by professionals and specialists in which children experience a routine of ever-changing, superficial relationships with teachers and classmates. This program teaches children some hidden messages: that no one really cares and that their life in this world is a "survival of the fittest" type existence. When these children become adults they naturally expect to experience the same types of shallow relationships.

God did not excuse Adam's actions. Adam's problem was spiritual. After looking closely at this subject, I believe it will be clear that the way that we relate to our children and how we educate them reflects our view of who and what God is and what kind of relationship we have with Him.

Our journey begins with an examination of two worldviews at war with each other, and the historic tension between these worldviews as they have battled for the heart and soul of the next generation.

CHAPTER TWO

Leaving Home:
The Decline of the Family

For the better part of the last two millennia, Western culture has been caught in the middle of a battle between two philosophies: The Greco-Roman worldview of man-driven priorities and the Christian worldview which is driven by the ideals set forth in Holy Scripture. The former emphasizes the autonomous reason of man and his eternal quest for personal philosophy, on the one hand, and social utility as defined by the State, on the other. The latter emphasizes obedience before God, a key component of which is the development of wisdom and godly relationships.

At times these philosophies have been merged and syncretized, with the results always being catastrophic. At other times, one worldview has prevailed over the other. But in every circumstance, the long-term prosperity of the nations which make up the West have been a function of their response to these two diametrically opposed philosophies.

At the heart of the Greco-Roman philosophy are two entities: the autonomous individual and the democratic state. Under this model, the individual looks after his own wealth and opportunities, leaving the state to develop the long-range plans for society. The state seeks to control the wealth and loyalty of the next generation. In looking to his own interests but ignoring the training of the next generation, the individual gains short-term satisfaction but surrenders the future. In fact, the more self-seeking the individual, the more the state is able to focus on controlling future generations. Ultimately, the centralized power of the State takes precedent over the individual and a generation arises that never knew freedom. It is this generation which willingly allows the State to control its private affairs in exchange for the promise that the state will supply sufficient benefits and stand in the place of the family when it comes to nurture and provision.

The foundational elements of the Christian order are the Church and the family. In a Christian worldview, the State is a limited, God-ordained institution designed to restrain evil and bear the sword against those who would harm families and individuals. It is not an instrument for social engineering, and the education of children is completely beyond its legitimate jurisdiction. The Church is the Bride of Christ on earth, and seeks to perpetuate and lead the many families and individuals which make up the people of God. The Church speaks for its interests through its institutional structures. But who speaks for the family?

This is an important question for the vitality of the Church. After all, it is the family that supports the Church and passes on the Christian heritage from generation to generation. The stronger the family, the stronger the Church; the stronger the Church, the more blessed the nation. But have Christian leaders effectively strengthened the vehicle needed to pass along a Christian heritage?

Here we see the fundamental tensions which drive this conflict. Passing along a heritage is an educational function. When fathers relinquish family responsibilities to the State or the Church, all institutions suffer, and especially the family. In the Greco-Roman model of society, the State is fixated on the goal of controlling future generations. Why is it that so few Christians care as much about the future as do the enemies of God? Shouldn't Christian leaders be thinking further ahead than the State?

The answer is an emphatic "yes," and the outcome to the present conflict will be determined by the way Christian leaders communicate vision for future generations, by the way they respond to the prioritization of the family in their lives, and by their choice of educational methodology.

The Decline of Greek Familism

Many have noted that the rise and fall of great civilizations follows an observable pattern. In order to establish a backdrop for considering the relevance of home education to the major concerns facing Christians today, it is necessary to briefly review the decline of familism in both Greco-Roman and Hebrew cultures. It is particularly useful to look at these early experiences since they foreshadow and shed light on our own. Later in the book we will examine the clash of these two cultures during the four hundred years preceding the first coming of the Messiah.

In the early days of Greek civilization, strong families, stemming from a robust religious heritage, were a central, defining feature of the culture. The chronicles of the poet Homer clearly bear this out. In *The Iliad*, Homer depicts a war fought over the desecration of family. Paris seduces Helen of Troy, wife of Menelaus, and the whole Greek world is at war over the violation of the sacred marital tradition. Likewise, *The Odyssey* is the story of one extraordinary man's love for his wife and child and of his long and perilous return to reclaim his position as husband and father. Just as Helen's unfaithfulness precipitates the Battle of Troy, so Penelope's fidelity to her husband makes Odysseus' homeward journey worthwhile.

In both of these tales, family ties are stressed in the names of characters and in the epic catalogs of heroes. Everyone is identified with father or mother—and sometimes with both. Homer intended his audience to understand the Greek world as nothing less than a family of families, interrelated by flesh and blood and held together by a common culture. Though Greek civilization often abused its power, the extended family provided protection and stability for its members that could not be matched by any other institution. These extended families were able to amass great wealth, as the hundreds of family members all worked to contribute to the well-being of the entire family. As these families prospered, their accumulated capital enabled them to venture into commerce with other families. To increase the efficiency of this commerce, families began to agree to abide by standards of commerce—law and regulations established by external institutions. Thus, the city-states of Athens and Sparta began to organize and develop governments. Intense competition over the jurisdiction and responsibilities of the family began to develop. As historian Carle Zimmerman observed of this period of Greek history:

> Family law and family religion suited a small unchanging agrarian society, but not a trading society, not an empire. There could be no increase of prosperity, no commerce, no division of labor without a conception of public law taking dominance over private law.[1]

But because people could see that commerce multiplied their wealth, they willingly gave up more and more family autonomy to the new governments.

As the people enjoyed the wealth they had accumulated, they tended to forget about their gods, give less attention to the family, have fewer children, and give more attention to the state, which to them was clearly the true benefactor of their prosperity. The laws ceased to protect the family as an institution and focused instead on the rights of *individuals*. In time, the extended family as a power ceased to exist.

As men gained greater independence from the family, women expected to be relieved of some of *their* domestic burdens as well. The care of children's minds—the most time-consuming responsibility in the family—was turned over to institutions outside the family and often to the state. In the quiet power struggle between the family and the state, the state welcomed the opportunity to train the children of future generations. This trend continued until the people finally came to view public control over education as essential for the future security of prosperity.

In his most famous work, *The Republic*, Plato proposed to dispense with the family altogether, turning the education of children over to a class of rulers whom he called "philosopher-kings."

> They [the philosopher-kings] will begin by sending out into the country all the inhabitants of the city who are more than ten years old, and will take possession of their children, who will be unaffected by the habits of their parents; these they will train in their own habits and laws, I mean in the laws which we have given them; and in this way the State and constitution of which we were speaking will soonest and most easily attain happiness, and the nation which has shown a constitution will gain most.[2]

It is important to note that the state which Plato hoped to establish was one in which property would be held in common, the role of women would be identical with that of men, and the private family would be abolished. And, for Plato, the education of children was the means by which this ideal state could best be ensured.

Free from their domestic responsibilities, women spent more time outside the home. Thus, the breakdown of the institution of marriage began to accelerate. Restrictions on divorce were lifted, and adultery and other sexual aberrations increased and became acceptable. After the family lost its power, all that remained was the all-pervasive, socialistic, democratic *government* and *individuals*.

In the final stages of this downward trend, children were left standing without the protection and provision of the family. Even custodial care of children became a public, instead of a private, concern. The role of the family was replaced by the state, and each person lived his life clamoring selfishly for his share of government services and rights.

As the philosophies of Plato and Socrates were accepted, Greek civilization turned from the family as the central, guiding culture force to an anti-familistic culture, represented by the individual and the state alone. It could be said that the Greek civilization committed suicide. When they destroyed the family, they destroyed the only institution that had any "spiritual" meaning to it, and that contained any meaningful *relationships*. Without this, there was no reason to bring children into the world. As a result, they could not even provide their armies with enough soldiers to protect their civilization. In short, without the family, they were dead.

The Greeks never took their gods very seriously. Of course, they had no reason to do so since there could be no relationship to gods that did not exist, except in their minds. Nonetheless, they did reflect their impersonal, warlike gods in the way they educated their children. The Greeks let the family decline as any other "outdated human institution." *Culture* is simply the religious values of a people lived out in a civilization.

The Greeks were not aware that their society was imploding, nor did they see the far-reaching implications they would experience for dumbing-down their family life. They could not see that an anti-familistic culture can never sustain a civilization. There were no Christians to stand up for the institution which God designed, so the family lost that historic struggle.

A Look at the Romans

The development of Roman civilization followed a path very similar to that of Greek civilization. Much of their history overlaps in time. Both began as religious, familistic civilizations which first organized their families into great estates. However, the Romans did not develop as quickly into a commercial nation. Before the Greeks began to influence them, Roman parents educated their children at home.[3]

They left commercial ventures and industry to the Greeks and other Eastern Mediterranean peoples.[4] Even during the height of their power, agriculture continued to be "the only occupation fit for a gentleman."[5] However, following the same pattern as the Greeks, this agrarian people eventually formed a republic, which evolved into an empire.

Prosperity caused the near-collapse of Roman civilization, even before the time of Christ. Roman self-indulgence and the reckless pursuit of pleasure brought on the collapse of the Roman Republic in 28 B.C. At that point, Caesar Augustus seized control and established the Roman Empire. He began his rule by instituting the reforms that alone are credited with preserving Roman civilization for another 200-300 years. The bulk of his reforms mandated a return to familistic practices.

Augustus had no Christian motivation in the institution of his reforms. However, he was perceptive enough to see that it was the decline of the family that had led to the collapse of Greece and was, therefore, concerned that his country was following the same path. Of serious strategic concern was the declining birth rate—he needed soldiers.

Augustus made no apologies for forcing his morality on others. He gave two speeches before the Roman senate explaining his motives in instituting his reforms. In a speech dated 9 A.D., Augustus praised the fathers of families and increased their advantages. He criticized the childless and increased the penalties against them. He claimed only "fathers" deserved to be called "men." He called the celibate and childless "murderers," "sacrilegious," and "impious." He also accused them of treason to the state.[6]

This speech came thirty-seven years after the reforms were first instituted. Augustus warned the people that if they did not start taking the reforms seriously, they were going to be treated as criminals and outcasts. A sampling of his reforms proves interesting:

- Among candidates for office, the one with the most children had preference.

- Of two consuls, the one with the most children became the senior.

- A relief from all personal taxes and burdens was granted to citizens who had a certain number of children: three if they lived in Rome, four if they lived in Italy, and five if they lived in the provinces.

- Unmarried persons could not inherit; married persons without children could inherit only half of the legacies left to them.

- It was a crime for a husband to refuse to divorce a wife found in adultery. (This was a stiffer penalty for adultery than in the past, when many husbands were indifferent to their wives' infidelity.)

During the last years of the Republic, the population continued to shrink, but during the thirty-four year period between 14 A.D. and 48 A.D. following the Augustan reforms, the number of citizens *increased* by 21%.[7] Augustus got his soldiers, and a revival of the Roman family occurred as a result of his reforms. The reign of Augustus marked the beginning of the *Pax Romana* ("Roman Peace"), which lasted for two hundred years. *World Book* says of this time that, "no country was strong enough to wage a major war on Rome, or to pose a serious threat to the frontiers. Commerce flourished, and the standard of living rose."

CHAPTER THREE

Greek Education and the Gymnasium

To understand the rise of the classical Greek model for education, one must examine the social development and transformation of family and state in the Hellenistic world. The period from the fourteenth to the ninth century B.C. is sometimes described as the "Trustee Period." For at least six centuries, Greek culture was primarily agrarian. Greeks lived as isolated, self-governing, extended families and clans. Family life was holistic, meaning that education, work, and even recreation took place in and around the life of the family. Children were essential to the success of the Greek family, and were integrated into every part of family life. Care for the mind and the body was provided within the framework of the family. Family rule was made up of traditions, religious beliefs, and family policies. In short, the early Greek family functioned as the social unit for civilization.

Whenever cultures promote and protect the God-created institution of the family, they experience prosperity. This is true regardless of whether a society is predominantly pagan or Christian. It is true because God's laws of success and blessing, each ultimately rooted in the doctrine of honor and obedience to lawful authority, are applicable at all times and for all people. It is equally true, however, that absent a moral compass pointing to faith in the one true God, the most "advanced" cultures are unable to manage their success or sustain the values which gave rise to their success in the beginning.

Prosperity must be matched by a multi-generational family vision or it will devolve into indolence, selfishness, and moral profligacy. Lacking a godly vision, the beneficiaries of prosperity view prosperity as an end in itself, or at least a means of promoting pleasure-seeking.

Commerce, efficiency, the accumulation of wealth, and the quest for greater comfort and entertainment ultimately drive the priorities of the society.

Like most rudderless societies, the Greeks were ill-equipped to handle their own success. They exchanged their traditional family-oriented attitudes and customs for new values deeply rooted in the philosophies of materialism. As interest in commerce developed, the Greeks began to organize around political and regional governments. Ultimately, the power of the clan was supplanted by the city-states. This trend marked the beginning of the second period of their history: the "domestic period."[1] Power, pleasure, and wealth assumed paramount importance. However, without the family to provide moral structure to society, the Greeks needed an instrument for bringing order and security to society. They found the answer in the highly organized political and military state. If the family could not do it efficiently, then certainly government could provide centralized and efficient order and cohesion to society.

Once the city-states gained preeminence over the families from which their civilizations had sprung, Greek leaders sought to educate the young people for military and political service to the state. By this time, the Greek family could no longer be described as "domestic." Sometime after 600 B.C. it became totally anti-familistic. Sons of Greek citizens—probably less than two thirds of the population— were now educated by the government. In the Greek city state of

Sparta, for example, family life was completely supplanted by a state-directed lifestyle. Boys, young men, and adults ate in community dining rooms. They were raised and trained by associations of adult males who assumed the role of both parent and teacher to the youth. Their priorities were defined by the priorities of the state.

The Greco-Roman Tutor

The Greeks did not rely entirely on schools for the boys' education. Many youths were taught by tutors. Later, the Romans would adopt this Greek tutorial system, but with an ironic twist. After conquering the Greeks, many Romans made them slaves and assigned them to be tutors to their children. William Barclay, in his book *Educational Ideals in the Ancient World*, writes that these "Greeklings" were slaves and men of no morals "whose effect on the boy would ultimately be harmful, and not good."² The slaves would take the young boys from teacher to teacher to be educated. Both Greeks and the Romans used this system in combination with the grammar schools, academies, and other secondary schools, which the Greeks and Romans are credited with developing.

The young boys struggled under the often harsh care of these tutors (*paidagogos*) until their fathers saw fit to release them from their schoolmasters. The Galatians were very familiar with this practice; thus, the Apostle Paul used it to illustrate to them the inferiority of the law in comparison to the New Covenant (Galatians 3:25).

The Gymnasium

Once a Greek boy reached the age of sixteen, he was to be educated in a "gymnasium." It was at the gymnasium that a boy would learn to become an athlete, a warrior, and a communicator. Students were trained to become the "guardians" of the people and were placed under the tutelage of an older citizen from whom they were to learn "virtue." The state controlled the system of education to ensure

uniformity of doctrine and thought. Especially important was the
need to train the Greek citizen-soldier to develop loyalty to the state
or the "Alma Mater" (literally, the "nurturing mother"). For this
reason, one of the first acts following the conquest of a city by the
Greeks was the establishment of gymnasiums. This practice was
enforced throughout the ancient world and even introduced in
Jerusalem.

In many respects, the gymnasium became the antithesis of the
biblical and Hebraic approach to education. Where Hebrew
education had stressed learning in the context of family relationships,
multi-generational training, and the fear of the Lord as the beginning
of wisdom and knowledge, Greek education and the establishment of
the gymnasium emphasized the development of the child as a
creature of the state who finds his identity as an individual, not a
member of a family.

Athleticism and the Worship of the Body

The first goal of the gymnasium was to take a boy and create the
fully-evolved, perfect physical specimen of the Greek man. Long
before Darwin ever penned *The Origin of the Species*, the Greeks
taught a form of evolutionism which emphasized man as a creature
en route to physiological and intellectual perfection. This idealized
Greek man would be both an athlete and a soldier, since both athletic
ability and intellectual prowess were considered the measure of a
man. Later, Nietzsche would adopt the Greek evolutionary ideal with
a vengeance in his work *Mensch und Ubermensch* (*Man and Superman*),
a book which helped fuel Adolf Hitler's vision for the education of
the student athlete, soldier, and superman of the future.

Academic and athletic competition were the cornerstone of the
Greek vision for training supermen. The worship of the body and the
exaltation of human reason were indispensable components of the
Greek philosophy. Their countless festivals and competitions were
driven by an intense religious passion for their pagan faith and

optimism in the perfectibility of man. It was in the context of religious worship and its relationship to athletics and culture, that the gymnasium was birthed. As Barclay puts it, "the work of the Greek is, above all things, the discovery of the individual."⁵ The Greek, then, was the *classic humanist*.

It is important to note that the very word *gymnasium* comes from a Greek word meaning "to exercise naked."³ The word athlete comes from the Greek goddess Athena, the goddess of wisdom, skills, and warfare. The Olympic games played a central role in Greek culture. Their calendar was based upon the Olympic cycle. According to *World Book*, "all the buildings in Olympia [the Greek city from which the torches of the modern Olympic flames are lighted] were for worship or for games."⁴ Their love for sports was a natural outflow of their understanding of the combative nature of their gods.

The Greek athletic and intellectual vision was enormously successful. Many cultures in and around the Hellenistic world would embrace this vision. At one point, even the Jews, the very people of God, actually petitioned the state to set up a gymnasium at Jerusalem in the immediate vicinity of the Temple. They petitioned the state, notwithstanding the fact that traditional Hebrew education—with its emphasis on a reverence for God, familial relationships, holiness, humility, and moral development—was the very antithesis of the Greek ideal, with its deification of reason and its glorification of the body. The Hellenization of the Jews contributed to cultural downfall and judgment. The hearts of children turned from their parents. After all, the gymnasium was much more attractive to the youth than the old fashioned relationship-driven approach to training with its emphasis on submission to authority, humility before God, and traditional wisdom. But the attraction of the gymnasium extended beyond just the Jewish youth. The author of the Second Book of the Maccabees provides this observation:

> And to such a height did the passion for Greek fashions rise, and the influx of foreign customs . . . that the priests were no longer

interested in the services of the altar, but despising the sanctuary, and neglecting the sacrifices, they hurried to take part in the unlawful displays held in the palaestra [wrestling arena] after the quoit throwing had been announced—thus setting at naught what their fathers honored and esteeming the glories of the Greeks above all else.[6]

The Hebrews had no biblical model of competitive athletics with which the Greek ideal could be compared. The fact that the Apostle Paul used a race to illustrate the dedication Christians should have towards God does not indicate that he was endorsing the Greco-Roman system of athletics, blessing nudity, or praising the gladiators (1 Corinthians 9:22-27). Paul does tell us that he kept his body *under subjection*, but that was so that his sinful flesh did not interfere with the spiritual conflict in which he saw himself.

The Hebrew father spent his time in a more serious endeavor—discipling his children and providing for his family. Hebrew "physical education" meant learning how to do useful work and serve others. The Hebrew vision for maintaining the body avoided both the Greek extreme in which the body was worshipped, and the Gnostic view that the body was evil because it was material. Jews understood that man had been created in the image of God. That he was given a physical body. Many of them believed in the resurrection of that body from the dead. Paul would later explain that the body was to be treated with respect and care as the temple of the Holy Spirit, but that physical exercise was not to dominate the life of the Christian: "For bodily exercise profiteth little" (1 Timothy 4:8).

By contrast, for the successful young Greek, becoming an elite athlete was an ideal to which he would aspire and for which he was willing to make great sacrifices to reach his goal. This these athletic ideals went hand in glove with a growing national obsession with highly publicized athletic events, like the Olympics, during which glory-seeking, pride, worship of the body, and immodesty were practically treated as national virtues.

There are enough contrasts between God's designs for "physical education" and the Greek system to suggest that the Spirit of God must have been sorely grieved when His people sought to build a gymnasium near His Temple in Jerusalem. God wanted His people to enjoy a close relationship with *Him* and close relationships in their families. His people rejected Him and chose the humanistic emphasis of the Greeks. So too, modern Christians should grieve to see the statues of naked gods and goddesses dotting many of our state capitals. They should remind us of the pride of man, his decadence, and the decadence of our own country in copying the pagan Greeks—their architecture, their educational systems, and their idolatrous worship of the body.

It is easy to see the connection between the rise of humanism in our country, the lack of understanding of the submissive character of Jesus Christ, and the corresponding obsession with superstar-driven, alcohol industry-subsidized, violence-laden sports in our culture to the detriment of the morals of our children and the focus of our family life. How it must grieve the Lord to see fathers looking forward to the weekly opportunity to sit before the television instead of before Him in church or leading the family in worship.

While modern athletic programs seem to meet some of the needs of star athletes, what are the lessons we teach to both the winners and the losers? The theme taught in modern athletic programs is not faith in God, but the basic tenet of the religion of humanism—the survival of the fittest. In this artificial setting, young people are learning that only the strong survive.

Frankly, it is difficult to reconcile the typical actions of so many of our "superstar" athletes with the fruits of the spirit, motivation of service, peace, modesty, humility, submission to the needs of others, and the example of the good Samaritan. In fact, there may be no aspect of modern culture which more perfectly reflects a quest for vainglory then the culture of professional athletics. By contrast, believers in the True God are commanded to:

Let nothing be done through strife or vainglory; but in lowliness of mind let each esteem the other better than themselves. Look not every man on his own things, but every man also on the things of others. Let this mind be in you, which was also in Christ Jesus Who, being in the form of God, thought it not robbery to be equal with God: But made himself of no reputation, and took upon Him the form of a servant, and was made in the likeness of men: And being found in fashion as a man, He humbled Himself, and became obedient unto death, even the death of the cross (Philippians 2:3-8).

Although athletics were totally foreign to Hebrew culture, they were not specifically forbidden in the Law, and they did not seem to *directly* infringe on any of their religious customs. Therefore the Jews did not understand the threat of the gymnasium or humanism until the Hellenization process was almost complete. Then, in 167 B.C., Antiochus Epiphanes desecrated the Jewish Temple with the sacrifice of a pig and rededicated the Temple in the name of Olympic Zeus. Many Jews had no problem replacing the sacred name Yahweh with Olympic Zeus, but others remembered the words of the Prophet Daniel and recognized the "abomination of desolation" (Daniel 8:9-14).

A Soldier for the State

Another purpose of the Greek gymnasium was to create an entire nation of soldiers who could serve the state and further its interests. The Greek athletic programs developed self-discipline and loyalty, though not loyalty to the family. These skills would then be applied with great success for the glory of the state. The Olympics were the showcase for these achievements. Thus, the ancient "Olympic dream" had as much to do with preparing warriors for the state as it did with athleticism.

The doctrine of the military state has long been with man. It was a critical part of the ancient world. City states like Sparta were the quintessential example of this statist and militaristic worldview. In contrast, the Hebrews were commanded to think in terms of self-government and decentralized state power. In fact, God had communicated to them that He did not want them to build their nation by following the example of the heathen nations. He told them not to desire a king to rule over them. Samuel warned them that the king would draft their beloved sons into the standing armies the king would need for defense (1 Samuel 8:7-20). He warned them that their decision would be costly to the family in many ways, and that they would be sorry once they had their own king: ". . . and ye shall be his servants. And ye shall cry out in that day because of your king which ye shall have chosen you; and the Lord will not hear you in that day" (1 Samuel 8:18). God gave them the desires of their hearts and from then on, God expected them to pay the price and learn to submit to an earthly king:

> For the eyes of the Lord run to and fro throughout the whole earth, to shew himself strong in the behalf of them whose heart is perfect toward Him. Herein thou hast done foolishly: therefore from henceforth thou shalt have wars. (2 Chronicles 16:9)

None of this Hebrew submission and humility before God could be found in the Greek character. Like contemporary society, the Greeks regarded such attitudes as weak and cowardly, the wrong-headed beliefs of a people destined to be slaves. The long history of God-granted victories by the Israelites would have puzzled and troubled them. Their gods were much less spiritual, much more human, much more dependent on physical strength and cunning.

Future Philosopher Kings

The final use of the gymnasium was for the development of oratory, which consisted not only of learning the techniques of voice projection and elocution, but emphasized logic and rhetoric. In the same way that the success of the modern lawyer is often linked to his ability to use technique to help him to successfully argue a case, irrespective of the moral truthfulness of his argument, so too, Greek students were taught to use rhetoric and logic as ends in and of themselves—tools by which he could demonstrate his elevated reason and abilities. After all, for the ancient Greeks, those who could not speak with precision and persuasion were considered the social equivalent of a barbarian.

In a biblical worldview, knowledge, logic, and rhetoric are not ends in and of themselves, but tools to advance the kingdom of God. True knowledge is the act of understanding reality consistent with the revelation of God. Logic is a reflection of the character of God. In the Bible, people spoke eloquently and persuasively because they learn to "think God's thoughts after Him," to reason with logic and precision from biblical presuppositions, and to stand strong in the confidence of the Lord. In fact, the Bible is the perfect manifestation of the logic of God, and the various communications we find in Scripture, from the inarticulate Moses and his well-spoken brother Aaron who stood before Pharaoh, to the brilliant Paul on Mars Hill proclaiming truth to the Greek philosophers, the Bible is replete with diverse examples of the ways in which God works through men of diverse abilities and skills to communicate His truth.

Scripture indicates that we are to "add to our faith virtue, and to our virtue, knowledge." It is this basic approach which ultimately distinguishes the methodologies of Hebrew education from Greek education as it applies to knowledge and wisdom. For the believer in God, the fundamental starting point for all training is faith in God, not man. The fear of God, and the complete acceptance of the fact that He is exactly who He says He is in Scripture—the beginning of all understanding. All academic wisdom and riches are deposited in Jesus Christ. He alone is the reference point (not the autonomous Greek mind of man) for interpreting all of reality and for growing in wisdom and knowledge.

Conclusion

The goal of Greek education was to raise children from infancy to be creatures of the State. The driving religious philosophy behind this system was the worship of man. The trades and all physical "work" were secondary to the adoration and development of the athletic body and the mind of man. Consequently, the success of the system was linked to its ability to produce world-class athletes. Such athletes received the highest respect and honor from the citizens and the state. In addition to the body, logic and reason—utterly divorced from biblical foundations—became the true objects of worship for the Greeks. Man and his autonomous reason were the measure of all things.

This Greek system only worked by removing children from their parents and handing them over to "experts" who were responsible for guiding the next generation. Their system *did* produce great knowledge, but it also produced pride, immorality, nakedness, institutionalism, dependence on government, a militaristic philosophy, and the destruction of family cohesiveness and love.

In contrast, godly educational systems are built on the foundation of the fear of the Lord. Thus, humility and education are inextricably linked. Only when men fear the One True God can they have knowledge, wisdom, or understanding. Every thought must be taken captive to the obedience of Christ, and the autonomous mind of man must be called what it is—a fallen, sinful, and imperfect tool which must be renewed by God before it can truly function properly. Logic and rhetoric find value insofar as they are derived from biblical presuppositions and used to advance holy causes.

Similarly, in a Christian and Hebraic approach to education, the body is a wonderful tool given by God to serve Him and to better take dominion over the earth. It is to be treated with respect, but it is not to be elevated to the point of worship. For this reason, Hebrew education emphasizes the equipping of the mind and body of man for the glory of God as an agent of dominion over the earth, but not the development of athleticism as an end in and of itself. The Hebrew method of training the full man takes place within the context of family relationship, discipleship, and personal training.

A tell-tale sign of paganism is nudity. Historically, a primary means for introducing nudity into a culture has been through athletic competition which emphasizes form, movement, and the prowess of the body. On the other hand, sensitivity toward immodesty or nakedness has been a characteristic of civilizations which understand the righteousness of God and the depravity of man. Christians should be wary of any educational process or cultural event (from locker rooms to swim events) which justify nakedness on the grounds of athletic freedom. Because much of modern education is driven by ancient Greek ideals, the Christian must be especially wary so that he can rebuild his educational philosophy on the one true Rock, Christ Jesus.

Can Christian young people be educated physically without teaching them to obsess on the Greek vision that athleticism equals success? The answer is a resounding "yes." As Christians build a distinctively biblical vision for family life, for involvement in the community and in the church, as they dedicate themselves to a life of service, they will find that most physical training takes place within the context of godly work and service to others. There are physical needs that are waiting to be met in almost every congregation and community. Families can learn practical skills while doing the physical work needed to meet needs and receive godly physical education at the same time (James 1:27). There is a place for recreation, but it is not to be a driving focus in our schedule, and certainly it is never to become idolatry. When we do engage in recreation, we must do so lawfully, which means an explicit rejection of the entire Greek philosophy of athletics. The true joy and happiness that will result and the testimony we can have before the world will more than replace any "fun" that the world has to offer (John 13:35).

CHAPTER FOUR

The Decline of Hebrew Education

God wanted the Israelites to live simple lives and trust in Him, not in their own abilities, technical or otherwise. The historian Nathan Drazin offers this insight into early Hebrew education:

> Jewish education was never something extraneous to life or merely an instrument that served to prepare for life and that could later be discarded when its utility was exhausted. Jewish education was rather synonymous with life. It unfolded life, giving it direction and meaning. In fact a modern Hebrew term for education, Hinuk, from a root found twice in the Bible in the sense of "to train" etymologically means dedication or initiation, and hence may refer to the fact that the child, on receiving Jewish education, was dedicating his life to the service of God and the observance of all His laws. This has been the characteristic essence of Jewish education from the earliest times.[1]

The Hebrew father enjoyed a personal relationship with his sons:

As arrows are in the hand of a mighty man; so are the sons of one's
youth. Happy is the man that hath his quiver full of them: they
shall not be ashamed, but they shall speak with the enemies in the
gate. (Psalms 127:4-5)

Hebrew fathers enjoyed the blessings of apprenticeship as their
boys grew older. It was normal for the children to work together as a
family (Genesis 46:7). God could have established a mass-production
educational system which would, no doubt, have been able to crank
out more facts per hour. But using home schooling, God would be
able to reach a higher goal than the impartation of knowledge. The
personal, relational, humbling, face-to-face process of education in
the home and by the family was the best context for producing love.

The Apostle Peter, a Hebrew disciple, understood the
importance of relationship in education. God designed an
educational process which would produce "heart knowledge," not
just "head knowledge." Even the word "training" denotes the need
for relationship—in contrast to the world's word "education."
Hebrew training began with relationship; its goal was perfect love:

And beside this, giving all diligence, add to your faith virtue; and to
virtue knowledge; and to knowledge temperance; and to
temperance patience; and to patience godliness; and to godliness
brotherly kindness; and to brotherly kindness charity. (2 Peter 1:5-7)

The world tends to forget about the necessary sequence for
education and focuses only on knowledge. To the world, it is not
important how one gains knowledge, so long as it is gained. In an
institutional educational setting, information is simply transferred,
without regard to faith or virtue, or the sequence given above. As a
result, knowledge puffs up (1 Corinthians 8:1-3). As more knowledge
is gained, pride becomes arrogance.

Humility was the hallmark of Hebrew education. Solomon, the
wisest man in the ancient world—a man who had the opportunity to

explore every pursuit in life—concluded the book of Ecclesiastes with this perspective:

> And further, by these, my son, be admonished: of making many books there is no end; and much study is a weariness of the flesh. Let us hear the conclusion of the whole matter: Fear God, and keep his commandments: for this is the whole duty of man. For God shall bring every work into judgment, with every secret thing, whether it be good or whether it be evil. (Ecclesiastes 12:12-14)

Josephus, looking back through his nation's history, recounts how faithfully the Hebrews followed this pattern. Commenting on the reliability of the ancient Jewish writings, he wrote:

> Because every one is not permitted of his own accord to be a writer, nor is there any disagreement in what is written; they being only prophets that have written the original and earliest accounts of things as they learned them of God himself by inspiration; and others have written what hath happened in their own times, and that in a very distinct manner also. For we have not an innumerable multitude of books among us, disagreeing from and contradicting one another [as the Greeks have,] but *only twenty-two books*, which contain the records of all the past times . . .² (Emphasis added, brackets in the original.)

Thus did the ancient Israelites guard against excessive pride in knowledge and also clarify the proper uses of learning. The mere twenty-two books recording the past of the Hebrew people were preserved because they contained the knowledge and wisdom necessary to remind the Israelites who they were and where they had come from. Contradictory accounts—volumes that challenged the validity of God's truth—had no place in Hebrew libraries because they did not serve the legitimate purpose of knowledge, which was to instruct a people in their relationship to God and to one another.

They avoided the temptation of allowing learning to receive the glory properly accorded only to God. This testimony is a monument to the humility of this great people.

When the Israelites needed special technical skill or knowledge, God gave it to them in a way in which man could not receive the glory. For example, it seems evident that the craftsmen who built the tabernacle never took engineering courses at the Egyptian schools while they were in bondage there. The Egyptians kept them making bricks so that they could not get ahead as a people. Yet, Israelite craftsmen—including metallurgists, highly skilled carpenters, chemists, and textile workers—were given the knowledge to perform their tasks in a special dispensation from God (Exodus 31:1-11).

Their greatest king and military leader, David, never attended military college or took formal classes in weaponry. Like most young men of his people, he tended sheep and learned the law. In 2 Samuel 22:35, he humbly attributed his great tactical skill to God's grace: *"He teacheth my hands to war; so that a bow of steel is broken by my arms"* (emphasis added).

David's son, Solomon, was known to be wise. People came from all parts of the world to marvel at his wisdom. But he had no university education, nor had he studied at one of the great classical academies. He simply asked God for wisdom, choosing that gift above riches, and, as the Bible tells us, "He was wiser than all men" (1 Kings 4:31).

Educated as a Pharisee and therefore full of great learning, the Apostle Paul nonetheless warns us:

> Where is the wise? Where is the scribe? Where is the disputer of this world? Hath not God made foolish the wisdom of this world? . . . For after that in the wisdom of God the world by wisdom knew not God, it pleased God by the foolishness of preaching to save them that believe . . . For ye see your calling, brethren, how that not many wise men after the flesh, not many mighty, not many noble, are called: but God hath chosen the foolish things of the

world to confound the wise; and God hath chosen the weak things of the world to confound the things which are mighty. (I Corinthians 1:19-21; 26-27)

The Clash

In 466 B.C., because the Israelites had strayed from the path of righteousness, God allowed the first temple to be destroyed by the Babylonians. Most of the Israelites who were captured and carried off to Babylon by King Nebuchadnezzar established roots in that foreign culture. Seventy years later, in accordance with God's plan, a remnant of people from the lower two tribes returned to Jerusalem to rebuild the temple. Though they left Babylon behind them, Babylon remained in their hearts. The troublesome times Nehemiah and Ezra had with this remnant are recorded in the books that bear their names.

Though the Israelites ultimately rebuilt the physical temple, they failed to rebuild the social and religious institutions which had given strength to their pre-exilic culture. The ancient Jews believed that the temple was the only place on earth in which God dwelt (in the Holy of Holies), and only there could priests sacrifice to God. During the Babylonian Captivity, with the temple destroyed, priests could no longer perform their priestly functions. So the exiled Jews established synagogues, "Sabbath schools," where the law was taught by a group of scholars later known as "scribes." The preeminence of the priesthood as the teachers of the law was never restored. The scribes took their place. And these scribes soon learned the ways of the Greeks.

From the response of the remnant to Ezra's first reading of the Law in the new Jewish settlement (Nehemiah 8:9-14) it is clear that these "Sabbath schools" were unable to keep the knowledge of Israel's heritage alive.[3] So when the remnant rebuilt the temple, the people did not know their heritage and did not understand the historic relationship between God and the Israelites. Thus they failed to trust God to lead them back to strength and righteousness.

This was the not the first time Hebrew leaders had faced such a problem. The generation that Moses brought out of Egypt soon forgot the Lord's faithfulness in delivering them from their bondage to Pharoah. For this reason, Moses had great difficulty controlling the people he led out into the desert. Likewise, the leaders of the remnant struggled to find ways of restoring the knowledge of their ancient culture. Historians don't even agree on what language the remnant spoke.

It is clear that the people understood the law when Ezra read it to them (Nehemiah 8), but after seventy years in captivity, with more than one generation reared in Babylon and influenced by Babylonian culture, it is reasonable to assume that they had forgotten much of the Hebrew language and many of the rules and practices of their forefathers. Further aggravating these problems, the people continued to intermarry with the surrounding heathen nations, contrary to God's prescription (Nehemiah 13:23-30). One authority writes concerning the language of the Jews:

> During the fourth century B.C., Aramaic became the spoken language of the Jews, leaving Hebrew as the written language of religious law. Since knowledge of Hebrew was necessary as a means of preserving the religious and national identity of the Jews, Hebrew became the major subject of instruction for those older boys who were to become the priests, scribes, and scholars.[4]

But even with such attempts to revive a lost culture, the restored Jewish settlement could not seem to escape the influence of the powerful pagan cultures that surrounded them. They returned to Palestine less than a generation before the Greek philosopher Plato began promoting his collectivistic society with its contempt for family and its enthronement of secular reason. Athens was enjoying its golden age, and pagan culture—later to be termed "classical"—was sweeping the world.

Eventually, out of fear of reprisal, the Jews virtually invited the Greek conqueror Alexander the Great to take over Jerusalem. The relationship of the Hebrews to the Lord of Hosts during this period was a far cry from what it had been in Joshua's time, when the people called on the Lord to deliver Jericho into their hands and the walls came tumbling down. They no longer trusted Him to deliver them from the hands of great and powerful enemies—hence the passive acceptance of Alexander's rule, with its strong pagan message. (Alexander, after all, had been tutored by Plato's greatest pupil, Aristotle.)

Even though Alexander died shortly thereafter, and his kingdom broke apart, the Jews continued to live under Greek cultural domination. After 150 years of this steady erosion, many Jews had turned from the law. They even abandoned their ancient and highly successful system of educating children in the home and built a gymnasium in the immediate vicinity of the temple in Jerusalem.[5] Josephus, in describing this period of great apostasy, writes that many of the Jews,

> were desirous to leave the laws of their country, and the Jewish way of living according to them, and to follow the king's laws, and the Grecian way of living: wherefore they desired his permission to build them a gymnasium at Jerusalem.[6]

In this way, the High Priest Jason, in support of the Greek ruler Antiochus Epiphanes and with the cooperation of upper class Jews, "conformed the young ephebes [students] completely to the Greek style of life by means of gymnasium education" (2 Maccabees 4:10). Education in the gymnasium included not only sports, but also Greek religion, philosophy, science, medicine, architecture, literature, oratory, and music—a liberal arts curriculum. The Jews who sent their children to the gymnasium were so enthusiastic about the Greek way of life that,

> they grew ashamed of the seal of the covenant of circumcision that was revealed to the gathering when they were naked during the games, and employed artificial means [surgery] to efface it.[7]

The goal of the reformers was "to transform the Jewish ethnos or the temple state of Jerusalem into a Greek *polis* [city-state], with a limited Greek-educated citizenry."

The successful Jewish Maccabean revolt was the reaction of the conservative Jews to Hellenization. However, after the death of Judas Maccabeus, the Hellenic influence reemerged.

> All the wicked, and those that transgressed the laws of their forefathers, sprang up again in Judea, and grew upon them, and distressed them on every side. A famine also assisted their wickedness, and afflicted the country till not a few, who by reason of their want of necessaries, and because they were not able to bear up against the miseries that both the famine and their enemies brought upon them, deserted their country, and went to the Macedonians [Greeks].

The Climax of History

Later, the Romans succeeded the Greeks as the world's most influential cultural force. Rome conquered and subsequently occupied the Middle East, and the Jews once again fell under the influence of Greek culture, since Roman civilization was highly derivative of Hellenic culture. The world was twenty-eight years into the *Pax Romana* when Mary and Joseph went to Bethlehem to be taxed and counted. By this time the Greek military and political leaders, with their logical and humanistic philosophies, had made a permanent impression on the captive Jewish nation.

Reforms notwithstanding, the Romans were carrying on many of the Greek traditions, including the Greek methods of educating children. Josephus gives an anecdote which illustrates the influence of Greek thinking on one of the leaders of the Jews. Speaking of Pistus, son of Jusus, who was trying to persuade the Jews to go to war against the Romans, he writes:

> [Pistus] exhorted the multitudes [to go to war]; for his abilities lay in making harangues to the people, and being too hard in his speeches for such as opposed him, though they advised what was more to their advantage, and this by his craftiness and his fallacies, for he was not unskillful in the learning of the Greeks; and in dependence on that skill it was that he undertook to write a history of these affairs, as aiming, by this way of haranguing, to disguise the truth.[8]

The cultural assimilation to Hellenism could be observed among the rabbis as well as the simple people. It manifested itself in their language and their appreciation of Greek philosophy, and even in their admittance of statues into their homes and synagogues.[3] To give one example, "one-half of all the young men in the house of Patriarch Rabban Gamliel studied 'Greek Wisdom.'"[9] Knowledge of "Greek philosophy . . . was tolerated by many rabbis and even considered a desirable accomplishment by some."

Many of the rabbis *did* struggle against the influence of the pagans. It would be unfair not to balance the picture given by the practices of other leaders:

> In the Talmud there is a story of a progressive young rabbi who wished to study Greek on the grounds that he had mastered the law. An older rabbi reminded him of the words of Joshua. "This book of the law shall not depart out of thy mouth; but thou shalt meditate therein day and night." Go then and consider, the elder

rabbi said, which is the hour which is neither of the day or of the night, and in it thou mayest study Greek wisdom.[10]

After the Maccabean revolt, the influence of Greek culture no longer took the form of a conscious acceptance of foreign ideas, but "consisted of a largely unnoticed absorption of the general atmosphere that prevailed in the world of those days."[11]

The scribes used the new scientific thinking skills they acquired in their dealings with the Greeks to develop an extensive commentary on the law, known as the oral law. Dr. Merrill Unger writes concerning the scribes:

> When under Greek influence, the priests, at least those of the higher strata, often applied themselves to heathen culture and more or less neglected the law, the scribes appeared as the zealous guardians of the law. From this time on they were the real teachers of the people, over whose life they bore complete sway . . . The scribes developed with careful casuistry the general precepts of the law; and where the written law made no direct provision they created a compensation, either by establishing a precedent or by inference from other valid legal decisions. In this way, during the last centuries before Christ, Jewish law became gradually an extensive and complicated science. This law being unwritten, and propagated by oral tradition, very assiduous study was necessary to obtain even a general acquaintance with it . . . The rabbis required from their students the most absolute reverence, *even surpassing the honor felt for parents*. (Emphasis added.)

The constant and perennial pressure on this small nation from almost every side eventually wore them down. Though many Jews tried to remain free from the foreign influence of paganism, it seemed impossible for them to avoid it. Thus, by the time of the "first century B.C., elementary schools were rather widely established outside the synagogues to give instruction in reading and writing to younger children." History records that the idea of a Hebrew public school system was first formally promoted by Shimon ben Shetah around 37 B.C.:

> Prior to that time, from Ezra [445 B.C.] to the Hasmonean period [142 B.C.-37 B.C.], a father taught his son the covenant law, for that act of teaching *was itself a covenant stipulation:* "And you shall impress them upon your children." Now the Pharisees, controlling as they did the internal affairs of the land, created a system of public schools. "All children must go to school," stipulated Shimon ben Shetah. A later Pharisee, Joshua ben Gamala, spelled out this general rule by specifying that each district and each town should have a free school for children. The covenant *and its oral traditions* could be transmitted most effectively *only in schools.*[12] (Emphasis added.)

Joshua ben Gamala, the Pharisee who established the Hebrew public school system, lived and remained influential until he was murdered in 68 A.D. For eighteen hundred years the Jews had not structurally altered God's law regulating the education of children. The Jewish leaders at this dark time in history now made it a law that Jewish children had to leave home daily and attend "houses of teaching" to learn the law at the feet of the rabbis who had made the new compulsory school law. With the additional requirements added by the scribes that the children also be educated in the complicated system of "oral law," parents were no longer deemed qualified to teach their children, *despite the law's injunction that they do so.*

The education the boys received in these schools was intensive in memorization of the law and the traditions. However, in the context they received this instruction—in the schools—*it did not produce life.*

God Calls the Fathers

It was in this setting that God sent John the Baptist to "turn the hearts of the fathers to their children" (Luke 1:17). The scribes had put themselves in a place that God had never designed for them— between God and His people, and between the fathers and their children. The people delegated *relationships* to professionals. Jesus summed up the spiritual condition of the Jews in Jerusalem for us, in Matthew 23:37, "Behold, your house is left unto you desolate."

In less than a generation following Christ's crucifixion, the decline of the Jews was in an advanced state. Consider this note provided by the translator of Josephus' works:

> Here we may discover the utter disgrace and ruin of the high priesthood among the Jews, when undeserving, ignoble, and vile persons were advanced to that office by the seditious; which sort of high priests were thereupon obliged to comply with and assist those that advanced them in their impious practices.[13]

When under pressure, the true heart of a people is revealed. Speaking of the Jewish leaders during Titus' siege of Jerusalem, Josephus writes:

> These men, therefore, trampled upon all the laws of man, and laughed at the laws of God; and for the oracles of the prophets, they ridicule them as the tricks of jugglers.[14]

The spiritual and familial relationships of this great family had reached their lowest ebb. Life for them had become cold and hard. History records that during Titus' siege and the famine in Jerusalem, the Jews even ate (I shudder to write this) their own children.

The fathers did not turn their hearts to their children; thus, the Jewish nation was not ready for its Messiah. They no longer knew the law as a *covenant relationship*. It had become an infinitely complicated system of irrelevant dos and don'ts rather than the description of a spiritual relationship with God (Matthew 15:3, 9; Matthew 23; Romans 7:14). And Israel's failure stemmed, in large part, from the failure of the Hebrew fathers to heed the educational mandate given them by God—a failure involving the very heart and soul of life and covenant: their relationship with their children (Matthew 18:5).

When God sent Jesus, the Hebrew of Hebrews, to them, "He came unto His own, and His own received Him not. But as many as received Him, to them gave He power to become the sons of God, even to them that believe on His name" (John 1:11-12). Jesus did not bring to them a new system of dos and don'ts. He came to show His people the importance of *relationship*. Consider His response when one of His disciples did not understand this point:

> Thomas saith unto him, Lord, we know not whither thou goest; and how can we know the way? Jesus saith unto him, I am the way, the truth and the life: no man cometh unto the Father, but by me. (John 14:5-6)

Jesus did not say, *"this* is the way," rather, he showed that *relationship* was at the heart of the Gospel message.

God designed the father-child relationship to teach this principle. God's people were not just to know about their children, but to know them as they "walked by the way" (Deuteronomy 6:7). They were not to delegate the education of their children to the scribes. Their refusal to receive the spiritual revival called for by John and embodied in the person of Jesus Christ resulted in the destruction of the Jewish civilization in 70 A.D.

Review of the Change in Jewish Education

In summary, a combination of several factors seems to have caused the Jews to abandon home schooling and turn to "public schools" as a means of educating their children:

1. The influence of Greek and other pagan philosophies on all the people, but primarily on the priests and leaders.

2. The complexity of the oral law, which evolved into a legalistic system under the care of experts, the scribes. The Jewish leaders actually replaced the written law of God with their own oral traditions (Matthew 15:3, 9; chapter 23). In this respect, they were disobeying the law as handed down from God to Moses and were forcing the people to do likewise.

3. The "statist thinking" that had become part of the culture at the time of Christ. In their attempt to replicate a Greek city-state in Jerusalem, the Jews encouraged a secular nationalistic spirit which made public education seem necessary.

4. The weak foundation of the parents who left Babylon to rebuild Jerusalem with Nehemiah and Ezra. The motivation for rebuilding Jerusalem originated more from a spirit of nationalism than from a desire to reestablish the covenant.

5. Language problems, particularly the discrepancy between the spoken language of the people (Aramaic) and the language of the law (Hebrew). Since they no longer understood Hebrew, Israelite fathers began to see the law as something foreign.

6. The physical extremities of the people—the never ending conflicts, wars, persecution, and economic duress caused by lack of dedication to their God.

One of the most unique characteristics of this period of Jewish history was that the family completely lost sight of its purpose, and the fathers turned their children over to schools for their education. Clearly many of these factors are present in contemporary American society.

How Was Jesus Educated?

Given that Hebrew culture was already in such a state of deterioration, and that Jewish leaders had experimented with the Greek model of education, the question naturally arises: How was Jesus educated? And more to the point: Was Jesus educated in a school?

This seems very unlikely. His parents were godly and truly kept the law. This fact by itself almost precludes the possibility that Jesus would have been educated in a school. The Jewish leaders were acting in disobedience to God's law when they started such schools. There is no mention in Scripture of Jesus being sent to school. Neither Peter nor John, two of his disciples, had been formally educated (Acts 4:13), so public schooling must not have been universal when they were young.

When Jesus went to the temple at Jerusalem, the scribes were amazed at His understanding (Luke 2:47). Had he been educated in one of the scribes' schools, surely the scribes in Jerusalem would have heard of this remarkable student before he reached the age of twelve. The recorded response of those hearing Jesus in the synagogue at Nazareth was, "From whence hath this man these things? And what wisdom is this which is given unto him that even such mighty works are wrought by his hands? Is not this the carpenter?" (Mark 6:2-3). Surely those in His home town would have credited the local school or a scribe for His wisdom had He been educated in one of the scribes' schools. He was referred to only as "the carpenter," "Joseph's son," or "the carpenter's son."

Additionally, Nathanael's incredulous response to the claim that Jesus was the prophet spoken of in the law, as expressed in his comment, "can any good thing come out of Nazareth" (John 1:46), confirms this point. People normally did not expect to see a person prepared for leadership come from Nazareth. It seems more than likely that Jesus was educated by His parents and apprenticed by His stepfather in the humble ways of the ancient Hebrews.

God's Law and the School

In the law, even with all the attention given to the regulation of daily living, there is no mention of schools. The education of children was of foremost importance. If there were to be schools when the Israelites became established in the "great and goodly cities" that God planned to give them (Deuteronomy 6:10), then surely there would have been some specifications given on how these schools were to function. The duties of the Levites, the future kings, the judges, and the elders were all described, but there was no mention of school teachers.

Schools were already in use by the Egyptians. Surely the Israelites, who had lived in Egypt for four hundred years, were familiar with these educational systems. Why is it that God did not simply pick up that institution and sanctify it for the Israelites' use? The question of why God did not choose to use the type of education that was already popular among pagan cultures around them for His people is an important one. We should ask ourselves the same question.

Conclusions

We were able to observe that the Greco-Roman civilization and philosophies, represented by a society organized as individuals and the state, cannot sustain a civilization. No matter how highly educated, or how well organized it is, or which people (Christians or non-Christians) depend on it, it only produces death.

Only the family can sustain a civilization. The family was created by God. In the same way that man is a spiritual creature, so is the family a spiritual creation. God uses it to bring human life into the world and to sustain human life after it comes into being. Each function and relationship of the family has been designed by God and has its own spiritual dimension. Each produces a happiness and fulfillment of its own if practiced in the context God designed. If physical intimacy is performed outside the marriage, it loses its spiritual meaning. If education is provided outside the family, it also loses its spiritual meaning. If a people by faith embrace the family as something sacred and spiritual, the family will uphold the people both inside the family and outside the family.

CHAPTER FIVE

The Development of the American Public School

When we talk about American schooling, different memories come to mind depending on one's age. Great-grandmother remembers the one-room school house. Her little brother was in the same classroom with her. She was called upon by the teacher to help him and his little buddies to learn to read. The school was near her home, and the teacher lived at home and went to the church on the corner. Great-grandmother tells us that her daddy was schooled at home, and that he could read and write well.

Great-grandmother can remember when her home state, Pennsylvania, adopted its first compulsory school law in 1895. "This law required that all children between the ages of 8 and 13 were to attend school *or be otherwise instructed* for at least 16 weeks in each year unless excused by a local school board. Pennsylvania became the first state to form an association of school boards."[1] The idea of compulsory education was not well received at first. The year following passage, the Pennsylvania Senate voted to repeal the law, but statism was gradually becoming accepted thinking. The Pennsylvania House of Representatives was also considering the repeal of the law until a young state representative stood up and electrified his colleagues with these words, "If the permanency of our government depends upon some knowledge, it is the duty of the government to see that the means of information be diffused to every citizen." The real motivation of the state of Pennsylvania was revealed by the arguments which convinced them of the need to keep the compulsory school law—to preserve the permanency of the government in power *at the expense of the family* which had controlled education up until that day.

Great-grandpa was pretty upset by this. He was keen on politics, and he feared where this might lead. But in time he grew accustomed to the idea, particularly since the teacher of the school was known to be of fine character (you should have seen the rules she had to live by to be a teacher) and was a member in good standing of the church on the corner. But things were not like they used to be. For some reason, children just weren't the same. Great-grandpa told about a booklet he had read, given to him by a friend at the factory. It was written in 1886, by the U.S. Assistant Attorney General, Zach Montgomery. Montgomery said in his report:

> It is maintained by multitudes of parents and many clergymen, while admitting that it is necessary that the consciences of children should be educated, that this education ought to be confined to the home circle and the church, and that the daily school should be exclusively reserved for the education of the mind and the body. But have we not seen that the conscience must be the governor and supreme ruler of the entire man; that the conscience must be taught the habit of governing, and that both the mind and body must be taught habits of prompt and willing obedience? But if, throughout the livelong day, the conscience is to remain practically dormant, while the mind and body are both in the process of active development, what will be the result?
>
> Is it not a universally admitted fact that every human organ,

whether it be an organ of the body, the mind, or the conscience, is strengthened by exercise and weakened by disuse? Then how is it possible that the conscience can maintain its supremacy over the mind and body if it is to be left sleeping or chained down in mute and motionless bondage, while the body and mind are daily growing in strength, activity, and habits of insubordination? *If, from the cradle to the grave, there is any one period of life more than any other when the conscience not only needs to be trained, but to be called into active service, it is during the time spent at school.* It is then that pride and vanity, and anger and lust, and all the other passions that war against conscience are in their most active state of development; and if instead of training these growing passions in habits of subjection to conscience, and instead of training the conscience to the habit of wielding its authority over these passions, the passions, on the contrary, be trained to lord it over the conscience, what must be the natural result? When a child has reached manhood, with passions fully developed and trained to command, and a conscience dwarfed and enfeebled by disuse, and trained to habits of base and cowardly servitude, what power, short of a miracle, can sufficiently restore the lost energy of such a conscience or give it the mastery over the entire man? But when the conscience has lost her sceptre and become the slave of the mere animal or intellectual man, then such a man lives only for the present life, and looks not beyond the portals of the grave, either in his search for happiness, or in his flight from pain. Such a man seeks happiness, chiefly, either in the gratification of his animal appetites, or in the acquisition of wealth, or in the paths of worldly ambition, marching to the music of human applause and grasping at the bubble of fame. (Emphasis added)

It made sense to Great-grandpa that "schooling" could not develop the conscience of a child since they sat still all day in class, and all they did was memorize and recall what they were taught. But school was only sixteen weeks a year (eighty days) and only met a half day at that. Surely there were enough things around the homestead to do so that Grandpop (a boy then) would have his character developed. Besides, Great-grandpa reasoned, he had spent ten years with his son, working on the farm together before he started a factory job. It would work out.

Great-grandpa had to admit, though, that what Mr. Montgomery had said in his book made a lot of sense. He had never really realized the fundamental difference between "schooling" and home education. He thought a lot about it and what he was hearing at church. Discipleship, he told himself, involves a continuous process of teaching and walking together—like a dad and his son—doing something together. It is not the same as sitting in a classroom, listening, memorizing, and recalling.

The booklet which Mr. Montgomery wrote included statistics compiled from the 1860 and 1870 census data, which demonstrated that the more money a state spent on compulsory school, the greater the crime rate and other social problems the state had. Mr. Montgomery reported:

> Here, then, in our humble opinion, is the true source of that alarming growth of suicides so prevalent in the United States. It is found in an educational system which has broken down parental authority, sundered the sacred bonds of affection that bound together brothers and sisters, parents and children, and which has weakened and almost obliterated the human conscience.[2]

Things have changed a lot since the good old days of Great-grandpa, even though only a little more than two generations have transpired. In between those years much has happened. America has seen two World Wars, many more women working in the factories (even after the wars), and greater industrialization. Schools began to take on a new role—that of day care. The school year was more than doubled in length (from 80 to 180 days) and in number of years (from age six to age thirteen).

By the 1960s, big changes were occurring in American education. Efficiency experts were working on consolidating the schools. Bigger schools were needed to keep up with the Baby Boom. Neighborhood schools were being closed, and the children were bussed across town to bigger schools. School buildings were much fancier, each with a beautiful gymnasium. After the Russians launched Sputnik, it looked as if the Unites States needed to mobilize as a nation and involve the federal government in education.

The sixties were tough years for young people and the family. For some reason many children seemed unhappy—even though it seemed that they had *everything*. Parents missed having the school down the street, but education was becoming costly, and consolidation seemed to be the most cost *effective* way to get the job done. Parents who wanted to be involved in their children's lives rallied around the public school, but it took a lot of effort to stay involved and keep track of what was going on there. Unfortunately, most parents were at the mercy of their children for information about what was happening in the schools. As a result, attempts by parents to play an active role in the public schools were thwarted—in part by the nature of the system, in part because an increasingly jealous educational establishment began to regard parents as "the enemy" and families as the repository of "old fashioned," and therefore, destructive ideas. At present, the hostility between parents and professional educators has become a topic of heated public debate. Indeed, for all practical purposes the two groups are at war with one another.

As we review this history, it is clear how the parent-child relationship has been pulled apart little by little. We cannot point the finger at any one generation, but we are waiting for some wise leaders to point to the better way!

Enter Christian Schools

As secular education became increasingly hostile to traditional social and moral values, Christian leaders found themselves faced with a decision. Clearly, they could not allow their children to be taught the things which were characteristic of the public school systems. Soon men who were trained to shepherd their flocks now found themselves being asked by their sheep to start "Christian" schools. With the limited experience they had had in the world of education, they stepped right into the task. We have to admire them for their courage. The secular establishment did not provide the new competition with much encouragement.

In Christian schools today, Christian school teachers *are* teaching the Bible and lessons from Christian textbooks; but they are following the structure established by the secular educational establishment. Many of them are struggling—especially with children whose parents are too busy to involve themselves in the school's programs.

Why are these schools struggling? I believe it is because the educational systems they have established are built on only one-third of the foundation they need to be successful. The foundation God designed for the education of children is the parent-child *relationship*. The mechanism God designed for the education of children is *discipleship*. The Greek system upon which the Christian educational system is built is missing both of these keys. The *subject matter*, Christianity, is taught, but without the proper relationship and mechanism, the program is encumbered from the start.

God gave the responsibility and the authority to train the child to the father. No matter how dedicated, the school teacher does not have the authority. She can try to fill the place of the parent during the day, but the authority for the training of children is a heritage given to those who brought the children into the world. The school teacher does not have the knowledge of the child or the soul compatibility; her authority is a delegated one. The child's loyalty is divided. He is trying to serve two masters. The school teacher's influence is spread over many students, and the relationship she is able to maintain with each child is minimal at best. Even the best school teacher serves many people: her own husband, her own children, the sixty parents of the children in her class, the thirty children in her class, the school, and in the case of the "hireling" (John 10:13), the paycheck. *Relationship* is compromised. God knew this would be the case. The home schooling father who has his priorities in line has none of these inherent problems.

For practical reasons, the *mechanism* (discipleship) is unavailable in a classroom setting. Since the classroom is an artificially contrived setting for young people, one teacher cannot expect to "walk along side of" thirty children. Discipleship is impossible. The most that can be expected from a classroom setting is teaching, memorizing, and recalling—activities of the mind. Character development is limited because the conscience is relatively inactive. There is less of a mechanism to deal with the carnal nature of the child than there is in a discipleship program.

When a church establishes a Christian school, the church, for all practical purposes, takes the place of the parents—a responsibility which is not the church's to take. There may be no intention to do this, but the Christian school actually hurts the family by usurping the family's God-given responsibility. Parents who would like to home school are sometimes even encouraged to "delegate" their responsibility and support the church school program.

The church has a responsibility to train *parents*, but there are few parent training programs being conducted in churches because little parenting is done at home. Older women in the church are left without purpose (Titus 2:4-5) because younger women are often not in their homes; and even if they are at home, the children are not there most of the time. School programs now absorb so much of most children's time that there is little left over for relationships at home. Children are often lonely and form improper relationships at school in an effort to satisfy the need God put in every person for a close family life.

When the public school student spends thirteen years of his life switching teachers, classes, and friends, what is he being taught about *relationships?*

- Is he being taught that life has enduring relationships which require commitment, or is he being taught to accept broken and shallow relationships, separation, superficiality, and abandonment?

- What is happening to the relationships between brothers and sisters when they spend so much time apart, in separate classrooms, with a separate circle of friends?

- By providing boys and girls with the same education, are we preparing them for the same roles in life—roles outside the home?

We have not been using this system for very long, so we can only speculate what the effects will be after a couple of generations. Furthermore, to what can we compare ourselves? At the turn of the century, the American divorce rate was already four times the average of eighteen other Western nations.[3] Those who want to see the statistics may compare the states which had compulsory school laws to those which did not in Mr. Montgomery's study. We cannot make such a study today because there is no population base in the United States without a compulsory attendance law in place. We can only study the system and speculate its effects.

There have been few times in history when children spent as little time in the home as children in this country do today. The effects of this system on the family in general have been devastating. God puts in children's hearts a natural desire for relationships with their parents. Children often cry and suffer from rejection when they are first put in school. Eventually, they adjust, and after a time they establish friendships in the schools. In too many cases the values of the children's close friends become more important than the values of their parents. By the time this happens, the real life of the child is at the school. Conflicts develop over whose standards the young people are obligated to follow: the father's, the mother's, the friends', or the school's? This trend can be checked by a close family relationship, but the danger is always present.

In later years, the family relationship is further compromised if the young person becomes involved in the school sports program, leaving even less time for genuine communion with parents. With involvement in sports, the home becomes little more than an airstrip for touch-and-go landings until the child graduates. In such an environment, what happens to the relationship between parents and children? It may seem normal and loving on the outside, but in truth the hearts of the children have been stolen by the schools.

Time for the Sabbath

The way of life God designed for His people supports itself in every way. There is no conflict within God's design. Each of God's institutions was designed in such a way that it does not diminish the importance of the family. God even set aside one day a week for the Israelites to spend together as a family—the Sabbath.

From sundown on the last workday in the week, until the same time Sabbath evening, God's people were to go home and rest (Exodus 16:29), reflect on the goodness of God over the past week, and worship Him. It was a prime teaching opportunity for the father. It also served as a weekly reminder that life was not based on survival of the fittest, but on relationship and faith. The Sabbath said, "trust in God to provide; look how He is providing!" Jesus taught that this special day was not to be observed as a mere legalistic requirement. The Sabbath was made for man's mental, physical, and spiritual refreshment (Mark 2:27; Isaiah 58:13-14). It was to be a day of sharing and hospitality (Exodus 20:10). It also served as a time for teaching— a time spent in every home preserving the spiritual heritage of the family.

Why do people today find it so difficult to "keep" the Sabbath? I believe the answer is obvious. Zach Montgomery mentioned the effects of developing the mind and the body in the classroom and school yard, while leaving the conscience, or spirit, dormant. Like the Greeks, we have developed the mind and the body, with little or no attention to the conscience (which we certainly have not nurtured in a discipleship program). Without exercise and nurture, the spirit is unable to control the mind and the body. Therefore, people who follow the way of the Greeks—either in passionate pursuit of technology, philosophy, and other learning, or in the development of the body through athletics—often find themselves unable to stop and set aside one day for their *spiritual* refreshment (Nehemiah 13:17-22). The spirit is too weak to control the other more highly developed parts of the person. As a result, there is little capacity to enjoy family worship and fellowship for a whole day.

Conclusions

Americans, even many Christian Americans, have come to view the family as a human invention to be redesigned and improved upon as we wish. It is time to return to the biblical view. It is time to restore the care of children's minds to the place God designed for it—the home.

Too many Christians have come to hold a utilitarian view of the ministries of the local church. If a support service which God designed for the local church is more conveniently available from the government or from an institution outside the local church, Christians often choose the government service, not remembering that this brings glory to the state (or some other institution) and *disrespect* for the church. Christian parent educators must turn their hearts to the local church. God is turning the hearts of parents to their children because He wants to build up *His church*. He wants home schooling parents to bring the love they learn from discipling their children back to the local church.

The shallow relationships between brothers and sisters in the extended family of the local church only reflect the weakness of the natural bonds between brothers and sisters in the homes. When a young person talks about his friends, he is not usually talking about his brothers or sisters. The real "life" of children is no longer lived at home; it is lived with unrelated friends at school. For the relationships of brothers and sisters in the local church to have the meaning that God designed for them, the family must be revived. For the words "love" and "forbearance" to have any real meaning, there must be more relationship between the members of local churches than sitting together for a couple of hours each week in worship. What is needed is a revival of the meaning of *relationship*. Home schooling is the key to this revival because it brings everyone back into the home.

CHAPTER SIX

Developing a Biblical Philosophy of Education

O nce upon a time in America, the family was the central building block of society. Today, the individual, divorced from the loyalties, obligations, and blessings of family life, is the heart and soul of our culture. The priorities of our nation have shifted from God-centered multi-generational faithfulness to self-centered individualism and egalitarianism. This shift in priorities is reflected in the culture which at every point is at war with the Christian family. The government schools, and all education systems which divorce training from family-centered discipleship, are at war with the Christian family. Hollywood is at war with the Christian family. The philosophy of the workplace is at war with the Christian family. The modern obsession with professional sports is not only a revival of Greco-Roman philosophy, but a direct assault on the Christian family. The sad truth is that rather than building a distinctively biblical approach to life, education, and work, the Christian community has been absorbed into the culture, such that the priorities of many of our local churches and church leaders are often at war with the Christian family.

Often, Pastors encumbered by heavy church debt and desperately hoping to encourage higher attendance through the creation of new programs, find themselves unwittingly advancing the anti-familistic spirit of the age. Even worse, their goals are sometimes pitted against the values of those parents who have experienced a revival of interest in the biblical model of the family. Many of these parents look back to the biblical commands from the book of Deuteronomy which were given to a people when family-friendly culture was waxing strong (Joshua 24:31). These parents say they want to obey these commandments *now*! No wonder there is a conflict! In just the past few years two cultures at opposite ends of the spectrum have met face to face. What are pastors going to do?

Thankfully, God has given Christians and the Church all that they need for guidance in faith and practice in the Holy Scripture. God's Word is not silent on this important issue.

God's Prescription for Education

The Word of God speaks clearly to the issue of the training and education of children in the Law, in normative patterns, like the example of Abraham, and in the very ministry of Our Lord Jesus Christ. We begin with the Law, because it is the perfect manifestation of the righteous standards of God and His very character. In the Law, the passage that is most often recognized as a biblical command for parent-directed, home-based education is Deuteronomy 6:6-7:

> And these words which I command thee this day, shall be in thy heart: And Thou shalt teach them diligently unto thy children, and shalt talk of them when thou sittest in thine house, and when thou walkest by the way, and when thou liest down, and when thou risest up.

Here we see the *who, what, where, when,* and *how* of education. It is important to note that the passage immediately follows what Jesus affirmed was the greatest commandment: to love the Lord with all one's heart. This educational commandment was central to the covenant responsibilities of Hebrew fathers. The commands that follow in verses eight and nine placed this responsibility ever before their eyes. It is therefore no surprise that the command to educate became one of the four scriptural passages Hebrew men wore in their phylacteries while they said their morning prayers.

Dr. Merrill Unger observes the following about early Hebrew education:

> We have no account of education specifically before the time of Moses. This much is certain that the mother looked to the training of the children in their earliest years (Proverbs 31:1; 2 Timothy 3:15), while the boys were trained by their fathers, or in well-to-do families by tutors (Numbers 11:12; Isaiah 49:23). This instruction was chiefly in reading and writing, but especially in the law. That reading and writing must have formed part of education from the very settlement of Palestine is evident from the fact that the Israelites were commanded to write the precepts of the law upon the doorposts and gates of their houses (Deuteronomy 6:9, 11:20); and upon their passage over Jordan, to write the law upon great stones (27:2-8), so as to be easily read by every Israelite. These admonitions unquestionably presuppose that the people could read plain writing (*q.v.*). Arithmetic must have been taught, as the days of the week, the months, the festivals, etc., were not designated by proper names, but by numerals. In fact, every art or science which occurs or is alluded to in the Old Testament, and upon the understanding of the Scriptures, must have to some extent formed a part of the strictly religious Jewish education. *There is, however, no trace of schools for the instruction of youth or of the people in pre-exilic times.* While there were no national or elementary schools before the exile, there were cases in which professional teachers were resorted to—when the position or official duties of the parent rendered his teaching impossible; when

the child's parents were incapacitated, or the child's attainments
surpassed the parent's abilities; or the son was preparing himself
for a different vocation from that of his father.¹ (Emphasis added.)

But what does this Scipture teach about the *who, what, where,
when,* and *how* of education? The *who* in the context of Deuteronomy
6 was the men of Israel, with the help of their wives (Deuteronomy
4:9-7:3). Where could parents hope to find help in fulfilling this
important responsibility? What about from the grandparents? Again,
in Deuteronomy 4:9, the prescription is quite explicit:

> Only take heed to thyself, and keep thy soul diligently, lest thou
> forget the things which thine eyes have seen, and lest they depart
> from thy heart all the days of thy life: but teach them to thy sons,
> *and thy son's sons.* (Deuteronomy 4:9, emphasis added.)

This instruction is found in other passages. Exodus 10:2 indicates
that the participation of grandparents in the education of children
was a cultural pattern even before the giving of the law. In fact, the
pattern was established even earlier. It is reasonable to assume from
the use of word "household" in Genesis 18:19 that Abraham helped
in the training of his grandchildren. Abraham had many children and
lived thirty-five years after Isaac married (Genesis 25:1-6, 21:5, 25:20).

In later scriptural passages, the advice is repeated. For example,
Psalm 71:17-18 speaks of the desire in a godly man's heart to teach his
grandchildren. The New Testament gives us an example of this
pattern in the discipling of Timothy by his mother and grandmother
(2 Timothy 1:5, 3:14). The impact of a grandparent's teaching can be
profound. What a powerful plan God designed! What purpose this
can provide for an older person's life!

Did the law mandate that education be provided exclusively by
parents and grandparents? Could parents decide not to do the
teaching? What if help is not available from within the natural family?
What about the examples described above by Dr. Unger? Did these

situations justify sending children to schools? According to Dr. Unger, sometimes professional teachers were used. But Scripture shows that while the ancient Jews sometimes employed tutors, they did so only under extraordinary circumstances (2 Kings 10:1; Numbers 11:12; Isaiah 49:23).

Note that some of the well-to-do Hebrews were too busy managing their wealth to be bothered with personally educating their children. Wealth also caused the Greeks to relinquish their family responsibilities. How can pastors build strong families today if they are encouraging parents to disassemble their families daily and send their children off to school? These contradictions and double standards point out the need for the extended family of the local church to reach out to today's families in ways that do not require that children be removed from the family setting.

What was taught to young Jews in the early days of Israel? We know at least one commandment that was taught. Deuteronomy 6:6-7 says, "These words . . . shall be in thine heart. And thou shalt teach them diligently unto thy children." This at least included the Ten Commandments, only one chapter earlier, and clearly should include all of God's Word. (As Dr. Unger points out, other things were taught as well, including the father's trade.) How many fathers have "these words" in *their* own hearts?

Where should the education of children take place? Two locations are specified in Deuteronomy 6:7. The context and the words "in thine house" clearly indicate that the primary place of education is in the parents' *own* home. But another option is also offered: "as thou walkest by the way." This passage indicates that education can take place anywhere the parent and child go together during the day. Thus can a young person be educated at his father's place of work and fulfill scriptural design, even if it is outside the home—as long as the *who* remains the parent or grandparent. The argument can be made that this verse actually mandates that parents should generally have children with them during the day. Otherwise, how could the parent fulfill his responsibility to teach?

The question of *when* instruction should take place is also answered by the Word of God. Deuteronomy 6:7 addresses three opportunities that exist in a typical day to teach children: "when thou sittest in thine house, when thou liest down, and when thou risest up." These occasions would naturally include those prime teaching times such as meal times and special times set aside for instruction. Mornings and evenings are ideal times for building memories and family traditions like praying together. In fact, this passage seems to suggest that there is no inappropriate time for teaching children from the Word.

The *how* of biblical education is summarized in the adverb "diligently." Teaching times are not confined to the home, but a father needs to be close to home in order to be a "type" or a godly father like Abraham. Diligent teaching should be taking place wherever the fathers are.

How long should this training process take? Some people believe their children are ready for independent missionary outreach in the public schools by age six, after receiving a Christian education from the church nursery, Sunday school, and Sunday church services. How many children are grounded in the faith before they reach kindergarten age? If you think, as I do, that very few are, then you might agree that we must be talking about Christian education for some years beyond ages five or six.

Are most children ready to stand alone by the time they reach puberty? I think it is interesting that Jesus did not begin His public ministry until He was thirty years old. He spent three full years with His adult disciples, and then He sent them out as missionaries two by two to reach the world. This is quite a contrast to the preparation little boys and girls receive before being sent out into the public schools to be missionaries. Children need to be discipled by their parents until they are grounded securely in the faith. For each child and each parent this process will take different lengths of time.

The simple life of the average Hebrew citizen did not demand any further education than that which could be passed along from the parents to the children. God's chosen people maintained a culture throughout their long and troubled history that made it possible for parents to fulfill these educational responsibilities. Parents should learn from this and evaluate the way their priorities impact their schedules. God through His Holy Word promised the Israelites that if they would love Him with all their hearts, keep his Word, and teach it diligently to their children, then they would as a nation enjoy success in every area of life (Deuteronomy 6:10-11). In fact, God's promise was that blessings would "overtake them" (Deuteronomy 28:2).

It is interesting to note that God makes the same promise to the heathen neighbors who surrounded the Israelites. If they would "diligently learn the ways of my people, to swear by my name, Yahweh liveth; as they taught my people to swear by Baal; then shall they be built in the midst of my people" (Jeremiah 12:16). The blessings of these teachings are available for our appropriation today.

The Hebrew Pattern of Education

Since before the days of Moses, Hebrew women have been famous for their dedication to the privileged role God gave them as mothers. In Moses' day, the Hebrew midwives explained to the Egyptian Pharaoh that the "Hebrew women are not as the Egyptian women; for they are lively" (Exodus 1:19). By "lively," they clearly meant energetic and active. This was not just a clever answer, but the characteristic of a nation blessed by the Lord (Isaiah 66:6-13). Hebrew women were uniquely successful in their matriarchal duties because they were educated to love and master this role (1 Samuel 1:8, 22; Psalms 127:3-5). Young girls were taught how to be physically, spiritually, mentally, and emotionally prepared for the birth, nurturing, and early education (training) of the children God would someday send them. Their education also focused on how to help their future husbands in fulfilling their roles of husband, father, and community leader and on the skills of successful homemaking (Titus

2:3-5). As Dr. Merrill Unger explained above, *mothers* provided much of the education for both boys and girls in their earliest years. Young boys then became apprentices under the tutelage of their fathers, and young girls became apprentices of their mothers.

Thus did God entrust to mothers—not day care facilities or nannies—the tenderest and most formative years of human life. The investment a mother makes in her relationship with a child and in the child's training during those first years largely determines the life of the little person and the strength and shape of the foundations of future generations (Matthew 25:14-30). The love relationship which bonds the child to the mother enables the child to trust others.

God has established the pattern and time sequence in creation for the education of children. The first six years of life present an opportunity that cannot be postponed. At no other time in the child's life is it as easy for the child to learn language. In fact, the child will never learn another language as well as the language he learns during those years. It is also a time when the child can absorb facts phenomenally. The Hebrew mother, in a loving and joyful way, cultivated a thirst and love for learning in her children and created the opportunities and moments in which to give them the treasures of knowledge.

The Hebrew mothers were diligent and creative in the way they taught their children. Hebrew mothers knew if they were not diligent in their training of their children, they as mothers would be brought to shame (Proverbs 29:15; 22:15). The Scriptures teach that when a woman serves her family well, her children and her husband will "arise up and call her blessed" (Proverbs 31:28). Hebrew mothers knew the importance of wisdom, language, and the Word of God (Deuteronomy 6:6-9).

To help the children learn to distinguish the letters that made up words, they baked cakes in the shapes of the letters of their alphabet. The children were taught to identify the letters before they could eat them. Some mothers were known to write out Scripture with honey and have their children lick the letters to taste the sweetness of God's law.[2] Their primary goal was to teach their children to read the Scriptures which the fathers wrote on the doorposts and gates of their houses. While the distinction between the mother's and the father's roles in the biblical Hebrew pattern is clear, the wife's role continued to be one of a helper to the father in the training of all children in the home (Proverbs 1:8).

At the time of weaning, the Hebrews believed the child to have reached a significant milestone in life, and this moment was frequently a time for rejoicing (Genesis 21:8; 1 Samuel 1:23-24). On the day that Isaac was weaned Abraham "made a great feast" (Genesis 21:8). Even for a busy man like Abraham, a man of extraordinary reputation, the weaning of his little son was a significant event. It signaled the beginning of a more active role of the father in his son's education.

The Hebrew father had three responsibilities: "to instruct his son in the law, to bring him into wedlock, and to teach him a handicraft."[3] By the time a son reached age thirteen, he was held responsible to know the law and to keep it.[4] Since the father was responsible for this part of his son's training, it is evident that the father's involvement started early in the life of his son. In fact, the Hebrew fathers began teaching their sons the law as soon as they were able to speak[5] enabling the son to develop a manly spirit.

Sons were to be prepared for leadership (Isaiah 38:19). As part of this preparation, three times a year a father was to appear with his son before the priest to hear the Word of God. Wives and daughters were also responsible to know and live by the law, but jurisidictionally, the men were held uniquely accountable for certain actions of the family. Consider, for example, that Numbers 30:2-16, makes it clear that male headship even extends to vows and contracts. The vow (or contract) of a wife or daughter, is only valid insofar as the husband allows it, or "ratifies" it by allowing it to stand in the day he hears of it.

The nature of Hebrew culture was such that family life, the education of the children, and work were inextricably woven together. While there was a rich diversity of occupations in Hebrew society, God's message to fathers, so beautifully articulated in Deuteronomy 6, was that they were to walk alongside and train their sons throughout the course of the day. This meant that though there may be an infinite diversity of lawful forms of labor and commerce by which a man could provide for his family and develop the strength of the family economy, his work could never be at the expense of the mandate to walk beside his children and train them in the way. Consequently, a man's occupation had to be inherently family-friendly, or he would be unable to obey the Lord as a father.

Perhaps this is one of the most important messages for men to consider today: It was important for a father to have an occupation that allowed him to spend time with his sons. Men must develop a lifestyle which allows them to integrate work, home, education and children. Parents who want to train their sons for biblical success, must begin by freeing them from the modern philosophy that the priorities of the "job" should drive the lifestyle of the family. The precise opposite is true. Wise parents will train their sons to develop skills with which they can exercise dominion over the earth for the glory of God, provide for their families, and walk in the way with their children for the purpose of training them and raising up another generation for the glory of God.

Lessons for Family Relationships

How were ancient Hebrew boys so well educated that they could know the law at age thirteen? A partial answer can be found in three characteristics from the preceding review: the specialization of the mothers and fathers in their roles, the father's early involvement, and the personal individualized training that Hebrew parents gave their children from birth.

The Hebrew pattern emphasizes differences in the education and roles of men and women. The world attempts to make their roles and education the same. It is understandable that the world takes an evolutionary view in this area, but why do Christians? It is as if we are saying that God did not know what He was doing when He designed His pattern for education. It is time we acknowledge that this was not an oversight. God wanted the training, thinking, and even the appearance (dress) of men and women to be distinct, because in His plan they have different roles (Deuteronomy 22:5). God's design for education would keep family bonds strong. In contrast to God's design, the Greeks wanted to weaken the family so that women could gain equal status with men in the name of *democracy*. Plato even suggested that they accomplish this goal by requiring both men and women to work out together in the gymnasium to eliminate modesty and the significance of the distinctiveness of the two sexes.

Implicit in the significance of the mother-child relationship is the importance of early education. Some modern educators recommend a "wait-and-watch" approach to education. The Hebrew mothers, however, did not wait for learning readiness in their children—they *developed* it. Much, if not most, of Hebrew training was oral (Proverbs 1:8). Even before a child can read, he absorbs tremendous amounts of information, and grows in knowledge and understanding as he listens to his parents. Parents can help children to learn by speaking clearly and repetitiously so that children will hear what they must hear. Parents can also help children learn to see (read) by using print which is large and clear enough for children to distinguish visually at their stage of development. Also, by reading the same words and stories often enough, parents can teach children to assimilate what is actually happening on the printed page. The ability to read may be more complicated than the ability to listen, but appropriate exercise will expedite the development of both. We don't wait for "hearing readiness," and, while we must not bully our children, we must not simply wait for reading readiness. To be effective, every parent must become knowledgeable in how children learn so that they can love and nurture their children without provoking them to wrath (Ephesians 6:4).

Because of the training Hebrew parents received, the help they received from wise grandparents, and the close relationship they had

with their children, discerning the appropriate rate of progress was a
natural process. Children's education was personal, face-to-face.
Their system of child training did not involve seating little children at
desks and asking them to sweat in independent study over workbooks
and textbooks written in tiny print designed for mature eyes.

I occasionally hear of parents who misunderstand the wise
admonition not to push young people too far too fast and have gone
to the other extreme of working very little with a child while they
wait for signs of awakening interest. Such parents fail to make the
distinction between "pushing" and "training or nurturing." Pushing is
coarse and overbearing and may overwhelm, provoke to anger, or
discourage. On the other hand, training and nurturing (discipling) is
pursued joyfully, with diligence, patience, and love. Passively waiting
is a form of neglect (Proverbs 29:15, 22:15). Biblically, parents are told
to *nurture* and *train* children—not simply wait for them to develop on
their own.

Ideally, both parents should live in such a way that they can
incorporate their children into the mission of the family and the life
of the household. But the life of a Christian household is more than
just cleaning and business, it is an entire culture devoted to giving
glory to God. This includes talking of God and telling His stories.
Parents must take the time to read or tell a story from the Word of
God, just as Jesus did (Luke 18:15). In this way they can cultivate a
delight in hearing the Word—and at the same time bring words to
life. Children should hear how great men feared the Lord and trusted
Him, how they demonstrated an excellent spirit, and how God
showed His love to His people (Deuteronomy 6:20-25). The
importance to the parent-child relationship of talking, cuddling, and
snuggling, cannot be over emphasized. This relationship is the key to
making education a delight. This way of life involves the
establishment of a high priority to time given to children. When a
father takes this responsibility seriously and gives of his time to teach
the Word to his children, the children are impressed with the
seriousness of God's Word.

Parents are stewards of the most wonderful treasure on earth—the lives of their children. Godly parents are motivated to develop it by love and stewardship, not pride. Children are born with an almost unlimited thirst for knowledge. They learn and absorb almost miraculously during their earliest years. The most teachable years of the child's life are primarily entrusted to the best teachers in the world—mothers. As stewards, parents must take advantage of the opportunity these years offer. The Hebrews did. We must not miss the opportunity that God provides for laying a deep, strong foundation of faith and learning that will last more than a lifetime.

Children must be trained thoroughly in God's Word so that they can stand alone for what is right before the Lord. Relational methods must be used for their education so that they will realize the purposes God designed for these relationships and not grow up and live independently of their extended families. Home schooling fulfills God's design for the education of children and the passing along of a godly heritage through many generations.

CHAPTER SEVEN

A Helping Hand Toward Home

Modern home educators are required to make numerous sacrifices in order to diligently work on rebuilding the family. I believe God is speaking to the hearts of many of these parents. They are recognizing that they need to do more than simply provide their children with an *education*. They are responding to the need to *disciple* them.

This is a difficult task in contemporary society. Home schooling was much easier in an earlier time, when families included grandparents and other relatives who lived in the same house or lived nearby and could help with the many responsibilities of homemaking and education. Today grandparents are living in retirement villages in Florida or California, and other relatives are scattered all over the country, pursuing their own lives, maintaining less and less contact with the extended family. Many parents are first-generation Christians, starting out from broken homes and in financial bondage. They need encouragement, training, and someone to help them keep the commitments they are making. Christian home schoolers are looking for help.

Home schoolers are "scattered" because of the huge division which exists between the family and the church today. "There is no shepherd" (Ezekiel 34:5). The vast proliferation of resources and assistance available from support groups, ministries, and publishers are very important, but they cannot possibly take the place of the primary organization which God designed for the care and leadership of Christians—the Church.

Christian home schoolers are usually associated with local churches, but thus far few church leaders have stepped in to provide the kind of support that home schoolers need. Certainly, one cannot expect the same pastors who encourage parents to subcontract the education of their children to government schools to also have a vision for the biblical model of education. Consequently, it is not surprising that many home educators sense that they cannot expect to find the sympathy, expertise, and guidance they need from such leadership.

In addition, church leaders already have a full plate. Pastors are struggling under the burden of counseling the growing number of people from broken families. The parents in their congregation are having trouble with their children. Marriages are collapsing under the pressures of modern living. Where will home schoolers receive the guidance they need as they begin the task of making disciples out of their own children?

Instead of viewing home schoolers as yet another distraction, shepherds should look at the opportunity their presence affords. God has already placed a burden in their hearts for the rebuilding of families. When parents become successful, the church will reap the benefits: men who are apt to teach, women who know how to love their children, and older women who will teach the younger women to love their husbands and children. The church will consist of people who have opened their hearts and lives to children and have allowed God to increase their capacity to love through the stretching process of learning how to love at home.

The Opportunity for the Local Church

The Church and the relationships in the Church are described in familistic terms ("household," "family," "sister," "brother," etc.). The supreme example of the familism of the church is found in the nature of the relationship between Christ and the Church, which is described as a marriage (Ephesians 5). It should come as no surprise, therefore, that God requires members of His Church to act like family members, one to another. Brothers and sisters in the Lord should operate as the "extended family" for those who do not have the help of a Christian natural family. The leaders of the Church should see themselves as the spiritual fathers and grandfathers of all the brothers and sisters in Christ (Philippians 2:22; 1 Timothy 5:1). It should be their hearts' desire to serve in this way and show love to children just as Jesus did. Just as the Church is instructed to help the widow without extended family to help them, so too the church should help single mothers to stay at home and educate their children. (1 Corinthians 12:22-28; 1 Thessalonians 4:9-12). In fact, leaders should actively motivate, train, and assist the men in their congregations for success as home educators.

When God designed the Church, He provided gifts so that the mixed body of Gentiles, who did not know the oracles of God, and His people, the Israelites, could unite and minister to one another in love. The Holy Spirit gave teaching gifts to the Church (1 Corinthians 12:28). These gifts are distributed to the entire body, men and women, young and old, but are to be manifested consistent with God's design for the family and the Church. For example, women who have teaching gifts are not to minister them before a mixed congregation of men and women (1 Timothy 2:11-15), but should follow the pattern established by godly women in the Old Testament. These gifted teachers were to exercise their gifts in the home, the younger women teaching their young children and the older women helping the younger women in teaching and homemaking (Titus 2:3-5). Because the American family is so fragmented today, churches are filled with adults of all ages who are not prepared to minister in these biblically-established patterns. The adults with these gifts must first be trained to use them.

Church shepherds are responsible to equip the fathers so that fathers can in turn shepherd their own families. Paul reminds us that pastors are responsible to see that everything in the congregation be "done decently and in order" (1 Corinthians 12:25, 14:34-40). It is therefore necessary that the shepherds of the local church administer these gifts (1 Corinthians 12:29). The goal should be that every child in the congregation is being properly discipled by his parents according to the pattern established by God so that the testimony of the Bride of Christ (Luke 1:17) and the Word of God be not blasphemed (Titus 2:5).

God is calling on His shepherds to prepare for His Son a bride who is pure in every way, including body, soul, and mind. Children must be discipled for God. This cannot happen if Christians allow the world to train the minds of the young people or if the Christian family loses sight of the primary task God designed for the home.

Jesus Christ Modeled Hebrew Education

Just as God, the Father of creation, had a desire to walk with Adam and Eve, sharing the wonders of His creation with them, so we should have a natural desire to walk with our children. The results of Adam's own "educational program" hindered the relationship Adam had with his Creator. As a result, Adam had to work among thorns and thistles the rest of his life. Today we are struggling with the thorns and thistles that have sprung up as the result of modern man's own attempts to find knowledge apart from the relationships God designed. That is why there is a need for more than just assembly line education. A truly godly society requires discipleship between earthly fathers and their sons. Just as God walked in the garden in the cool of the day and called out to Adam, "Where art thou?" (Genesis 3:9), so modern fathers must learn from our Heavenly Father, asking God to touch our hearts and give us the desire to walk with our sons. We should not be saying to them, "I am too busy to talk with you now." We should be saying, "Where art thou?"

Because the Hebrew fathers knew in their hearts that God wanted them to personally teach their children at home and "while they walked by the way," Jesus was able to prick their disobedient hearts by drawing attention to His intimate relationship with His Heavenly Father. Notice the extent of the Son's dependence on the Father, the Father's motivation, and the extent of His involvement in His Son's training illustrated in the following verse:

> Then answered Jesus and said unto them, Verily, verily, I say unto you, The Son can do *nothing* of Himself, but what He seeth the Father do: for what things soever He doeth, these also doeth the Son likewise. For the Father *loveth the Son, and sheweth Him all things that Himself doeth.* (John 5:19, 20, emphasis added.)

Discipleship implies more than just teaching, as our Savior demonstrated in His earthly ministry. He might have opened a school for his disciples if He had chosen, but He knew the only way to prepare them for the special mission He had in mind—to make them His *disciples*—was to *walk along side them*. Jesus had more than just ideas to communicate to His disciples. Mere ideas can be found in books; such knowledge can be transmitted and then tested, like the multiplication tables and verb conjugations. For the task He had in mind, however, Jesus knew He had to spend countless hours with his disciples, even to the point of weariness. Do we have such a vision for what we want our children to do with their lives? We should. And if we do, we should devote enormous amounts of time to them, even to the point of weariness. It is in this fashion that fathers are commanded to disciple their children.

Jesus taught His disciples by example that both their lives and their time were important. He taught them diligence by rising early in the morning to ask for help from His Heavenly Father. He taught them that following the ways of God can be painful and dangerous, even life-threatening. Parents must teach their children the same lessons by example—by emulating the life of Jesus, the greatest teacher and discipler on earth.

The primary lesson Christ taught His disciples through His life was a living message of love from His Heavenly Father. He admonished His disciples not to worry about their physical needs, but to "seek ye first the kingdom of God and His righteousness, and all these things shall be added unto you" (Matthew 6:33). Do we believe what He said? The challenge for fathers is to disciple our children the way Jesus discipled His "children," and watch where God leads them.

Turning our hearts to our children is a humbling experience, one that God has designed for us so that we might be fit for our Master's use. We all fall short in every way. We do not know God's Word as we should; we have grown to trust in human institutions, building our whole lives around them. We have been missing the primary discipleship program God designed for His people long before He established His Church—a program ministered in the home. As we follow God's pattern for the education of our children, we will discover a whole new world of challenges for spiritual growth.

Knowledge and Submission: The Essence of Relationships

In 1 Corinthians 8:1, Paul teaches that "knowledge puffeth up, but charity edifieth." This passage and its context remind us that we must never allow the knowledge we have to be the cause of another brother's stumbling. In educating our children, we must seek to establish loving relationships, not merely the transmission of knowledge. The depth of any human relationship dictates which knowledge can and should be shared. God deals with us in this way. He only reveals to us knowledge that we should have and can bear (Genesis 2:17). Knowledge is, therefore, to be prized only inasmuch as it enables us to better love and serve our Lord, our family, and our neighbors. Knowledge that does not lead to wisdom (that is, seeing things from God's perspective) promotes pride—not glory to God. Wisdom received from above is gentle and peaceable. It does not produce strife or a proud, competitive spirit (James 3:13-18).

The proper role of knowledge is to nurture our relationships with God and other people. Knowledge of the gospel brings us into a relationship with Jesus Christ. It has been said, "To know Him is to love Him, and to love Him is to serve Him." The greater knowledge one receives, the greater the ability and the responsibility one has to use that knowledge to serve others. This principle encompasses not only "religious knowledge," but all knowledge. Service involves obedience and submission to the will or needs of another. In fact, the essence of all human relationships is the attitude of submission—for both those under authority and those in authority (Luke 22:24-27).

Let it be further noted that godly submission in no way involves weakness. Rather, godly submission is making a courageous decision to serve. Following our Lord's example, a husband is not only expected to "submit," but, dying to self, he models submission for his whole family. It takes knowledge to know how to serve. Where better than in the home can a godly response to authority and submission to one another be learned? Where better to acquire the practical training in the submission of children to parents, parents to children, wives to husbands, and husbands to wives (Ephesians 5:21-33)?

A father must *study* the needs of his children so that he will not provoke them to wrath (Ephesians 6:4). The apostle Peter teaches in 1 Peter 3:7-8 that husbands must study the needs of their wives so that they can "dwell with them according to *knowledge*" (emphasis added), care for them as a weaker vessel, and avoid offending or discouraging them.

Husbands readily note the passages of Scripture that speak of a wife's responsibility to submit to them. Yet, they often overlook the passage admonishing *all* to "by love *serve* one another" (Galatians 5:13b, emphasis added). The word "love" (which husbands are required to exercise toward their wives) embodies all of the "submissiveness" in the word "submission"—and much more. Love "seeketh not her own" (1 Corinthians 13:4). Jesus Christ, the head of the Church, is the example of submissiveness (Ephesians 5:25; Philippians 2:2-8; 1 Peter 2-4). This principle was so important for the success of the people of God that the Lord directed the ancient Hebrews that for the first *year* of marriage, a husband was to avoid all other business and make his wife happy (Deuteronomy 24:5).

King Solomon wrote, "The fear of the Lord is the beginning of knowledge" (Proverbs 1:7). So fundamental is this submissive attitude in life that the only commandment given to children is that they honor and obey their parents (Exodus 20:12; Ephesians 6:1-2). A submissive attitude must be "walked" before children as well as "talked." While parents are expected to correct their children when they fail to obey (Hebrews 12:7-10), a self-centered or self-willed father will most likely reap only envy and strife in his home because of his own poor example. If by his example a father fails to teach his young children their only commandment, what has he taught them? He has taught them that the important things are unimportant.

Our joy in the Lord is in knowing that He died for us, and that He lives for us today! In the Garden of Gethsemane, our Savior painfully considered the needs of those given to His care and the task that was set before Him. He asked His Heavenly Father if there were any other way possible to restore the relationship between God and man. He knew it was His Father's desire for His sheep to experientially know His love. Therefore, Christ was willing to die to His own will and live for us. Today He is our High Priest and our Good Shepherd!

Happiness and joy are multiplied in homes where fathers make the same decision—to die to self and live so that those committed to their care can experience what Christ-like love is. When a father dies to self, he also gives up a critical spirit and gains a new desire and ability to build up, praise, and encourage—to edify. He becomes a nurturer (and will probably have to chastise less frequently as well).

Submission to Civil Authority

The same principles apply outside the home. A man must submit to the overseers in his local church (Hebrews 13:17), to his employer and employees (Ephesians 6:5-9), and to the government if he is to bring glory to God. Though he had personally received unjust punishment from the Roman government (as did our Savior), Peter commands believers to "submit yourselves to every ordinance of man for the Lord's sake" and to government officials at all levels (1 Peter 2:13-15). Sometimes the demands of petty government officials make life difficult for us, but liberty demands that Christians focus on their *responsibilities*, not their rights (1 Corinthians 8; Matthew 17:27).

Satan wants to destroy the testimony of Christian parents by making them appear angry, overly cautious, isolated, fearful, and even superstitious. How must we respond to a hostile power? We must not live in fear but, by wisdom, have faith that God will provide "a mouth and wisdom which your adversaries shall not be able to gainsay nor resist" (Luke 21:15). However, we cannot expect God to bless an angry or bitter spirit (Hebrews 12:15).

Before God can use these pressure situations to bring glory to His Name, we must learn to have an *excellent spirit*. An excellent spirit begins with a biblical outlook. The principle of submission to authority is rooted in the law (Deuteronomy 17:9-13). We must fully appreciate that those in authority are being used by God as ministers (Romans 13:4). This principle of submission even applies when the leaders oppress us (1 Samuel 8). We very often do not know what God in His sovereignty is accomplishing by keeping them in power, but we must guard our spirits and not forget that these men are God's ministers (Jude 10). We should follow the example of our Savior and go out of our way not to offend them (Matthew 17:27).

Daniel provides us with an outstanding example of how God blesses an "excellent spirit" (Daniel 6:3). Believers who display the inner qualities of submission, faith, and knowledge are often given the opportunity to preserve their nations by actually helping ungodly leaders enact good laws, as illustrated in the biblical accounts of Joseph and Esther. The morning after Daniel was placed in the lion's den, the heathen king came out to see if Daniel's God had been able to deliver him. Daniel could have cited the injustice he had just endured at the hand of the king. Instead, his first words were, "O king, live forever" (Daniel 6:21). Because of Daniel's excellent spirit and God's deliverance, King Darius published the Hebrew gospel (the good news about Yahweh) throughout the land (Daniel 6:25-28).[1]

Young David, a properly home-educated lad, demonstrated his excellent spirit by refusing "to speak evil of dignities" as he was pursued by Saul, an unjust king whose heart was full of unjustified hatred toward him. David's submissive spirit in the face of such persecution is recognized as messianic (1 Samuel 18-30; Jude 8-19).

Church leaders (and government officials) are watching home schoolers to determine what kind of spirit is in their hearts. Home schoolers should not simply withdraw from or shun the programs that overseers work to provide for their people, not without carefully communicating their motives to those whom God has put in authority over them. Otherwise, these leaders are likely to interpret their actions as coming from an "independent spirit." This perception can make it more difficult for other home schoolers to be received in the congregation in the future.

It is proper for home schoolers to keep legislators informed about what God is doing in their hearts as well. Like Elijah, legislators can lose faith in the family if they do not hear from the righteous (1 Kings 19:14, 18). So much of the time they hear only about the failures of parents.

The Apostle Peter provides us with a wonderful study on submission. He holds up Sarah's submissive spirit as a model for all of us (1 Peter 3:6-7). Even though Sarah was put in a difficult position by her husband (Genesis 12 and 20), she submitted to him and trusted God. She was not alone, however, because, as the Apostle Peter reminds us in the same context, "The eyes of the Lord are over the righteous, and his ears are open unto their prayers" (1 Peter 3:12).

We have focused on the father because *he* is the teacher of these important truths. To determine how well educated a man truly is, one can observe to what extent the man loves and lives to serve and please his Lord, wife, children, extended family, brothers in Christ, and others his life touches.

Great knowledge requires great submission. Great submission requires great knowledge. The message of the gospel is that the One who had the greatest knowledge died to Himself and served all of mankind. In Him is "hid all the treasures of wisdom and knowledge" (Colossians 2:3). He taught us God's design for knowledge and the secret which gives meaning to life—having a servant's heart (Luke 9:23-24). A godly education will be designed around these principles.

By application, home schooling families can demonstrate that what they are learning in their homes is true "knowledge" by looking for opportunities to serve other brothers and sisters in the local church and looking for ways to meet some of their basic needs. Families can win the hearts of their pastors by keeping the unity of the local church a high priority, balancing it with other reachable family goals. Church unity is important to our Savior and a priority of every pastor (John 17).

The Legacy of Grandparents

The Social Security Act of 1935 signaled a change in roles for America's grandparents. God designed a reciprocal plan for the care of the weak and frail—both young and old—*inside* the extended family. According to that plan, as the aged surrender the burden of supporting the family, they are in turn cared for by their adult children. But this isn't the end of their responsibilities. Their experience is extremely valuable to the whole family and most particularly to the little ones. Grandparents can provide dimensions of purpose in life, seriousness, and stability that young parents cannot (Titus 2:2). God doesn't intend that the experience of a lifetime be wasted. He intends that such wisdom be passed along directly to the grandchildren. I have come to believe that God purposely slows the elderly down to make them available to fulfill this role.

Unfortunately, even though the teaching responsibility of the elderly is as clearly described in Scripture as the responsibility of parents, Christians seem to be more directed and bound by the priorities of American culture than the biblical model of family (Deuteronomy 4:9, 6:7; Titus 2:2-3; 1 Timothy 3:2; 1 Peter 3:5-6). The absence of this teaching has affected the life of the church as well. Recently, a pastor expressed his frustration with the elderly in his congregation. He explained to me that though many of the older men in his congregation were qualified to serve as elders, they were unwilling to do so because they were in retirement—off to Florida nine months of the year or just too busy with their own lives to fulfill the responsibilities God designed for them.

Many grandparents no longer look to the family for either their provision or life purpose. They are characterized by independence, individualism, and financial dependence on the government. To many, government social security programs have become more sacred than the family. Ask any politician. The government can meddle with the family, and only a few people react; but for a politician to even suggest tampering with Social Security is political suicide.

In the late 1800s we saw the rise of compulsory public school attendance requirements. One generation later we saw government social security. What we are seeing (after little more than a couple of generations of anti-familistic culture) is the truth of Dr. Raymond Moore's statement, that "the earlier you institutionalize your children, the earlier they will institutionalize you." When the elderly finally do need physical care, where do they receive it—in the homes of family members or in nursing homes?

In the meantime one need only look at the younger generation and consider their lack of life purpose, seriousness, and stability to witness the hidden costs of the American system of social security, as well as the cost of sending children outside the home for their education. With children in school all day, what opportunities are there for grandparents to exercise their God-given responsibilities?

Christians must return to the relationships God designed for the family. Where no grandparents are available to serve in this capacity, the elderly men and women of the family of believers in the local church must work to fill this need.

CHAPTER EIGHT

Steps in Rebuilding

God has created a pattern to rebuild familism, a series of steps that a church home school ministry can help set in motion. The order in which they are listed may not have any significance. They are simply a reversal of the steps that historically have led to decline. Every shepherd should seek the Lord for wisdom and develop his own plan. No two church home school ministries need necessarily be alike.

God is turning the hearts of parents to their children. But God is specifically calling for the hearts of *fathers*. During the five-year period I was working to help home education receive legal recognition under Pennsylvania law, I received many phone calls from parents concerning a wide variety of problems. For every twenty calls I received, I estimate that only one was from a father. The responsibility for home education in the Church Age still remains chiefly with the fathers (Ephesians 6:4), but until recently the modern home education movement has been largely borne by the mothers.

It seems that men are often content to let someone else assume their familial responsibilities for them. So far, many fathers have been willing to allow their wives to take on the task of home education. The process itself has not had a serious impact on the lives of most men. The modern home school movement is therefore a type of "women's movement"—and the women have done a great job. However, biblical home schooling is chiefly a responsibility of the father. The Scriptures and history make this clear. Today, too much of this responsibility is delegated to the wife. County home school support groups cannot correct this problem because they have no authority to do so. It requires shepherds who understand what the Bible says about the education of children—shepherds who accept their own responsibility to hold the men in their flocks accountable for fulfilling their duties in this all-important area (Matthew 18:10). If overseers will not lead in this area, home schooling within and without the local church will remain a program for the mothers, thus falling short of God's design.

A Mission for the Local Church

There should be at least three major thrusts to a local church's home education ministry: First, the ministry of the local church should emphasize accountability for the men. For those who see no need for accountability, I recommend a devotional study of the book of Judges through to the last verse. When a man is persuaded in his heart the Word of God teaches that the education of his family is his responsibility and he affirms this to the overseers of his local church, the overseers in turn have a responsibility to disciple this man so that he can be faithful to his convictions. The wife is accountable to her husband. There must be a regular program to ascertain the faithfulness of the father. As he becomes known for his faithfulness, he can be counted among the faithful men (2 Timothy 2:2) and begin discipling other men. In this way the church can build upon a solid foundation of faithful men. One of the difficulties churches face today is the question of how to determine the reputation of prospective leaders. This problem must be solved in a biblical fashion (Titus 1:6; 2:6-8).

Second, the church should focus on *support* for both mothers and fathers. This support includes, for the women, help provided by gifted lady teachers and older women (Titus 2:2-5). For the rest of the congregation, training in principles of child rearing should be provided.

The third emphasis should be building an *involved* church leadership. The leaders overseeing this ministry will need to work as a brotherhood, ministering to one another as well as to the whole flock. In a church that is truly preparing its people for the coming of the Lord, these leaders need to meet regularly. It is difficult to imagine that they could oversee a growing, living congregation by meeting less often than once a week.

In the following steps for rebuilding, I have focused primarily on the men. God's standard of righteousness is the example of His own Son, who gave His all for His sheep. Every one of us falls short of His standards, and, experienced home schooler or not, we are unprofitable (Romans 3:12). It is with this thought in mind that we should consider the following steps. Home schooling, as all dads will learn, is a continuous lesson in humility. God designed this for us.

1. **Fathers must heed God's call, and begin to rebuild God's institution, the family.** Proclaim the call of the prophet Elijah and John the Baptist to fathers to turn their hearts to their children. God's design for men is that, through their relationships with their children, they make the love of the Father believable to the children. Fathers must see what America has done to the family and personally ask God for grace and the repentant heart needed for the rebuilding process to begin. We have trusted too much in the institutions of men, not in God and His institution, the family. If we don't repent, we will continue to follow the pattern of the Greeks. Statism and individualism can sustain neither the Church nor our families. If we will not turn to God and His precise design for the family, we will experience decay in our families and churches just as our nation now is experiencing decay in its political institutions.

Sometimes God speaks to the mother's heart first, but before real rebuilding can occur, God must touch the heart of the father.

Many in the congregation must see the need for renewed commitment, because the parents of childbearing age will need lots of encouragement from those who do not have children. With a limited extended family to assist parents who seek to rebuild the family, the local church family must chip in and help.

Signaling a return to the home, it would be wise to make *hospitality* and *discipleship* high priorities. Many families today are in bondage not just financially, but also to their jobs, to their careers, and to relationships. They need to be delivered. We should remember that we were all in bondage once, and that the One we follow sacrificed His all to free us. The rebuilding process calls for a renewed dependence on God and casting off our trust in man's institutions. Though the rebuilding process may take years for some, it can be an exciting time of spiritual renewal.

Men whose hearts are turned will be expected to make commitments to practice their convictions and show a willingness to obey those who have the rule over them. The overseers who are responsible for every soul in the flock will someday give account for the souls under their care. The overseers must hold men accountable for the way they lead their families.

> Obey them that have the rule over you, and submit yourselves: for they watch for your souls, as they that must give account, that they may do it with joy, and not with grief: for that is unprofitable for you. (Hebrews 13:17)

Men should willingly submit. However, if they do not, the elders might do well to note how Nehemiah handled such situations (Nehemiah 13:25).

There may be other costs. A man's decision to turn his heart to his family may cost him much of his spare time. It may require him to give up his hobbies. It may even force him to change his occupation. These things a man cannot take with him into the next life. But he can take his family. His decision will be rewarded in heaven.

In summary, this step involves a man hearing God's Word regarding his responsibility to his children and making a decision to become a doer.

2. Receive and learn to love the children God wants to send. Many of us do not love children the way Jesus showed us He loves children. It is time for us to recognize what people really mean when they say, "I love children—as long as they are other people's children." As a consequence of this attitude, we do not love each other as Jesus loves us. Without children in our homes there will never be a rebuilding of familism. There must be a call for obedience to the first command God gave to man: be fruitful and multiply. A new love for children is needed for this step to occur. We must ask God to give us a new love for the children God wants to send into our lives.

Parents should be willing to receive the children God wants to give them to stretch their capacity to love. As God gives parents a new love for children, the parents' hearts will begin to accept their responsibility to educate them. People, young and old alike, must be touched with a love for children if they hope to be Christlike. If children are not loved and wanted by many in the congregation, there will never be any support for the development of parent-training courses in child discipline, nurturing, and other training that will be necessary for the rebuilding of the family. It would be wise for churches to teach the grandparents their responsibility to their grandchildren. This will touch the hearts of many and provide great encouragement for everyone.

3. Women must find their way back home. Women must return to the primary role God designed for them: helpmeets to their husbands, keepers at home, and mothers to children (Proverbs 31; 1 Timothy 5:14; Titus 2:5). They must learn to love their own children and obey their own husbands (Matthew 6:24). This point is pivotal. If this way of life is not restored, the testimony of the Church and the Word of God will continue to be blasphemed. Many women have not been raised to love and cherish the role of mother. Even Christian colleges tend to prepare women for careers outside the home. Young women and mothers need help. One of the greatest losses is the fact that the Christian community is suffering because we have lost an entire infrastructure of help and support for families which was historically provided through the single ladies of the congregation.

God will raise up women in the Church who will have a unique ministry of helping the young mothers. This is especially important for the first generation of rebuilders. The role of these women is to coach, train, and encourage (Titus 2:4). If there are no women qualified in the Church to serve in this role, the church leaders should ask God to raise up a sister with the gift of teaching who can stand in the gap, who can be trained to help the mothers who have children.

Part of the rebuilding process is learning how to make the home a delightful place to be. Much of American home life has become dreary. Mothers need to relearn how to make the maximum use of their homes as worship centers, hospitality centers, and education and craft centers. Some of these craft centers will no doubt become platforms for the development of home industries. Often these home industries are the first steps toward deliverance from the many forms of bondage in which today's families find themselves. Leaders can also help single mothers develop home industries.

4. The local church must instruct fathers in their responsibility to educate their children. Fathers must bring their children back home for their education. This is a matter of obedience to the Word of God to His peculiar people (Deuteronomy 6:4-9).

Especially for their very young sons, fathers need to work to personally provide new role models of what it means to be a man— a family man. Little children love to act out the roles of their heroes. Young people need heroes. Unfortunately, the world has not held up the family father as the "real" man. We need to remove the images of Davy Crockett, Clint Eastwood, Elvis Presley, John Wayne, Rambo, and Homer Simpson as role models and replace them with the picture of a godly man who is faithful to his family. Fathers should study the lives of Job and Abraham—the great men of history.

Then fathers must help their sons to make wise decisions in the big choices of life—what their occupation should be, whom they should marry, and where and how they should live. Fathers must ensure that their sons are prepared for these responsibilities when the time for them arrives. If a son is ready for marriage in his heart but not ready to support a wife, the father may have fallen short of his responsibility.

God's people must rediscover the "family" of the church into which God has placed them. Instead of looking to the world for our roots, we need to reconstruct our whole view of where we live—as members of the body of Christ—*not* as citizens of this world. Our brothers and sisters are *in the Church*. We should expect to find help there and be willing to show brotherly kindness to our brothers in need. Our lives are cluttered with outside institutions competing for our time, resources, and loyalty. Church-hopping, an independent spirit, and lack of commitment (love) for the other believers in our local bodies are sinful attitudes which diminish the effectiveness of the local church.

5. Reevaluate the father's priorities. The father must put the priorities of his occupation in the proper balance. The occupation must not be the focus of either parent. We must change our view of what a father is. He is not just a breadwinner. Commerce is not his main purpose in life. He is a *nurturer*. This word implies a much broader scope of responsibility (Ephesians 6:4). Most men have little vision of what a nurturer is. A godly man must see his jobs and "career," not as ends in and of themselves, but as part of a larger dominion mission of service to the Lord, of which the training and discipling of his family are at the core. Everything else will pass away, but his investments in the lives of his children will last for eternity. God will provide for the needs of the family through the diligent work of the father. If the father loves his job more than he loves the Lord or his family, he has his priorities out of balance. If his attention becomes focused on prosperity, the father is involved in idolatry. Many fathers are in bondage to their jobs—this is the god they serve.

Often the choice of an occupation involves the choice of a place to live. The agrarian life of the Hebrews offered an ideal setting for raising up new generations. God gave His family, Israel, a wonderful land in which to live. This land was given so that they could have a safe place to rear their children. The rearing involved educating in God's law, finding their sons the right spouse, and providing each son with a handicraft. A good piece of land can help a father accomplish all these worthy goals, but he must take care to approach it with wisdom. Be cautious, however. Christians are not limited to living in rural areas. God also promises his children "goodly cities." Consider also that while land is a solid asset which can be passed along to future generations, its availability may be limited or beyond the immediate reach of the family, especially for those who hope to build a godly future debt-free.

The great Rechabite family avoided the ownership of property for more than two hundred years because one of their patriarchs feared it would limit their success as a family (1 Chronicles 2:55; Judges 1:16, 4:11; Exodus 3:1; 1 Samuel 15:6). The Rechabites were successful in avoiding the trap of setting their affections on things of this world because of their father's foresight. As a result, they were not taken into captivity when the Assyrians defeated Israel, and the Rechabites were delivered from the Babylonians when they defeated the southern tribes.

Land ownership can also be a distraction to those who are in the ministry. God wanted the Levites to trust in Him and be ministered to by the people they served. The Israelites remained largely a pastoral people even until the Babylonian captivity. Their constant straying from God teaches us that the pastoral way of life in itself is not the solution. We know that God also promised the Israelites "great and goodly cities" for their blessing (Deuteronomy 6:10, 28:3).

We can see many things God designed for our blessing, prosperity, and safety, including all of His designs for the family and the land of Israel. But these things in themselves will never sustain us unless we love the Lord our God with all our heart, soul, and might. On the other hand, if we truly love Him, we will seek to live in accordance with His designs.

It is important, therefore, if a man decides to live in a "great and goodly city" (assuming he can find one) that he select a family-oriented commercial or industrial business. He must also learn to view capital as a trust from God to the family. This attitude will be a challenge. A small town might be a wiser choice if commerce or industry is the man's trade. Individualism and an independent spirit chip away at the health of the family. In 1947, Carle Zimmerman wrote: "It is very difficult to reconcile 'family' and the 'individualism' necessary to an industrial, urban, and yet highly warlike and nationalistic society such as ours."[1] We may not be as warlike as we seemed to be during the 1940s, but the truth of what Mr. Zimmerman says is still valid.

A pastor and I recently consulted with another pastor to learn how it was that 75% of the men in his sixty-family assembly worked in home-based businesses. He explained that the brothers in his assembly met monthly to share counsel, finances, and experience to help one another get established. Since the start of their church, his vision has been: "I believe that God wants the men home." He said, "I believe that if they will pray and be patient, God will bring them home." An exciting two-hour discussion followed.

We must remember Lot and examine our motives before "pitching our tents" toward the pagan cities of American culture. Yet God has sent pious men into cities to call people living there to repentance. Examples of these servants are Jonah and Philip, the evangelist. Both of these men established godly communities within the cities to which they were sent. Doing this takes a man who can stay close to God and who is definitely called upon to have such a ministry. There is no indication in Scripture that Lot was "called" to go to Sodom. It takes a man better prepared than he to be able to survive in such a city.

Sometimes the most humble occupations provide hidden benefits to a man. This was the case for the Israelites as they went down to Egypt for help. The Egyptians despised shepherds, so they gave the Israelites land and left them alone for a long time. Sometimes occupations that seem attractive have hidden pitfalls. Holding important positions in government can produce conflicts in a man's priorities. A man's own family can seem less important when he is responsible to lead many others. King David and Joseph both experienced unique preparation for the challenges they would face as men in high government positions. God provided them with years to learn how to meditate on God's faithfulness—David as a shepherd and Joseph as a prisoner. It should be noted that a heart full of the love of commerce, high technology, or material things has little room left for meditation on God's word.

People whose lives are almost taken over by the excitement of challenging and creative occupations face unique temptations. The absent-minded professor who forgets his anniversary and the man who has made his wife a "computer widow" illustrate this occupational hazard. Large corporations with heavy capital investments often pressure their employees to sacrifice their family lives or their ministries in the local body of Christ for the sake of advancing their careers.

Sometimes it may be wise to step away from the lure of such occupations. On the other hand, computers are opening up new opportunities for occupations at home. There is nothing inherently wrong with efficiency or technology, but they, like great riches, present unique challenges which many men cannot successfully face. That is why Solomon cautioned us not to seek to be rich (Proverbs 30:8). If we know we will have a tendency to put a particular occupation first in our lives, we should consider it a youthful lust and flee from it. We should approach our occupations with these thoughts in mind.

Ye see your calling, brethren, how that not many wise men after the flesh, not many mighty, not many noble are called. (I Corinthians 1:26)

Finally, we must allow contentment and patience to be our guides as we venture down this road. If changes are needed, we may have to wait a long time for our freedom from bondage. The Israelites found themselves in this situation for many years before God delivered them from Egypt. They were shepherds in their hearts but had to make bricks from mud and straw for a long time before they were delivered. For some men, deliverance may not come in their lifetimes. God knows our hearts, our frames, and how much we can bear. Pastors must be sensitive and allow God to work in the hearts of men. Other brothers in Christ must not judge, but must encourage and be willing to help each other to make the needed changes. These are not easy decisions.

In 1947, Carle Zimmerman, whose scholarly book *Family and Civilization* has been so helpful in this study, predicted that those committed to the institution of the family

> cannot move from job to job, purchase new automobiles every year, live in the fashionable sections of their communities, or do a thousand things the others can do, simply because their energy is largely absorbed in the rearing and training of the next generation. They cannot be the "smart" people, because they have responsibilities of a more serious nature.[2]

6. Cultivate a new understanding of capital. The capital God provides must be viewed as a trust from Him belonging to the family, not the father, or any individuals in it (Leviticus 25:10, 23). Fathers must search out the biblical pattern of passing along the inheritance to their children (Numbers 27:8; Deuteronomy 21:15).

> And it shall be, when Yahweh thy God shall have brought thee into the land which he sware unto thy fathers, to Abraham, to Isaac,

and to Jacob, to give thee great and goodly cities, which thou
buildest not, and houses full of all good things which thou filledst
not, and wells digged, which thou diggedst not, vineyards and olive
trees, which thou plantedst not. (Deuteronomy 6:10-11)

7. Recognize that God designed the family—but God is first.
We must thank God for all His blessings and vow never to turn from
following Him (Joshua 24:15). Our love for the Lord must be first:

Thou shalt love Yahweh thy God with all thine heart, and with all
thy soul, and with all thy might. (Deuteronomy 6:5)

Our love for our Lord must be so great that our love for our
family members must be like hatred *in contrast*:

If any man come to me and hate not his father and mother, and
wife, and children, and brethren, and sisters, yea, and his own life
also, he cannot be my disciple. (Luke 14:25)

Then beware lest thou forget Yahweh which brought thee forth
out of the land of Egypt, from the house of bondage. Thou shalt
fear Yahweh thy God, and serve Him, and shalt swear by His name.
(Deuteronomy 6:12-13)

CHAPTER NINE

A Safe Course Lies Ahead

The commitments church leaders make in the areas of family and the education of their children are some of the first fruits the world examines when it seeks to verify the sincerity of the spoken Christian testimony. Unfortunately, the world sees Christians acquire and manage their resources no differently than non-Christians. It sees no major differences in family relationships.

I would like to mention the reaction of one angry, but famous unbeliever who observed that many people pay lip service to the importance of relationship to education—they say they care about the family—but really only care about economic prosperity:

> The bourgeois clap-trap about the family and education, about the hallowed co-relation of parent and child, becomes all the more disgusting, the more, by the action of Modern Industry, all family ties among the proletarians are torn asunder, and their children transformed into simple books of commerce and instruments of labor.[1]

Karl Marx was born into a home with a religious heritage. He knew what Christians said they believed. I have mentioned how important it is for Christians to view capital as a trust from God to the family. Because people did not follow this principle in Marx's day, he could see the inconsistencies of a society in transition, moving from a familistic society, which had used home education, to an urban, industrial, non-familistic society, which was changing its view of children and beginning to depend on schools for their education. Marx reasoned that the communists should not be accused of trying to eliminate home education because the people had already forfeited home education voluntarily.[2]

In spite of the utter bankruptcy of the ancient Greek society, Western universities and the education establishment elites continue to embrace their democratic ideals and philosophies as means to heaven on earth, with the best of mankind in control. American thinking has changed. Pastors cannot be passive followers. They must wake up and herald a biblical philosophy of child training for their sheep.

God created man. The needs of man did not change at the start of the Church Age. He created the family as the institution to meet most of man's human needs. He designed the family and put the responsibility for the care of children's minds and bodies in the family. God's design is clear for all those who have eyes to see. We have a choice: either we have strong families and little sin, or we have weak families and lots of sin. We do not have the option of redesigning the family according to our desires. The direction we are headed right now is clear: we are following the Greeks to the grave. But if we will stop depending on their systems, including their man-made methods for educating children, God can bless us with life. The relationships He designed will begin to come alive in the home and in the Church.

If we want our churches filled with godly women like Sarah and men qualified to be elders (1 Timothy 3:3-7; Titus 1:6-9), we must commit ourselves to rebuilding the family. If we want to see "a people made ready for the Lord" (Luke 1:17), we must commit ourselves to establishing home education under the local church. May we say with David:

The law of the Lord is perfect, converting the soul: the testimony of the Lord is sure, making wise the simple. The statutes of the Lord are right, rejoicing the heart: the commandment of the Lord is pure, enlightening the eyes. The fear of the Lord is clean, enduring for ever: The judgments of the Lord are true and righteous altogether. More to be desired are they than gold, yea, than much fine gold: sweeter also than honey and the honeycomb. Moreover by them is thy servant warned: and in keeping of them there is great reward. (Psalms 19:7-11)

Blessed is the man that walketh not in the counsel of the ungodly, nor standeth in the way of sinners, nor sitteth in the seat of the scornful. But his delight is in the law of the Lord; and in His law doth he meditate day and night. And he shall be like a tree planted by the rivers of water, that bringeth forth his fruit in his season; his leaf also shall not wither; and whatsoever he doeth shall prosper. (Psalm 1:1-3)

Home education is not an end in and of itself. It is a God ordained means to a biblical end: The training of the child after the image of the God who made him; the building of the family; and the promotion of a multi-generational legacy of faithfulness. One of the great blessings of home education is that the very act of intensely involving parents in the education of their children facilitates the process of elevating the home and the family to the place which God designed for them. Similarly, church directed home school ministries are not ends in and of themselves. They do, however, ultimately build the very infrastructure of the Church by restoring its family foundations, and restore respect for the body of Christ by demonstrating that Christians can have a testimony of strong family life because the biblical patterns for such a life are honored.

The Fruit is Hospitality:
Early Church Evangelism

As the family is restored, the ministry of the household becomes stronger and stronger. Strong families mean effective evangelism. A powerful context for evangelism that is readily accessible to every family is the ministry of hospitality. Hospitality provides an opportunity to show that faith produces more than just talk. It produces *works*—expressions of love from the very place where love is learned—the Christian *home*.

> Therefore all things whatsoever ye would that men should do to you, do ye even so to them: for this is the law and the prophets. (Matthew 7:12)

> For I was an hungred, and ye gave me meat: I was thirsty, and ye gave me drink: I was a stranger, and ye took me in. (Matthew 25:35)

Gregg Harris, a nationally-recognized spokesman for home education and director of Christian Life Workshops, has written an excellent book entitled, *The Hospitality Handbook*. Explaining the link between evangelism and hospitality, Mr. Harris writes:

> Viewing hospitality as a context for evangelism and fellowship helps us understand why Paul wrote as he did to the young Christians in 1 Thessalonians 4:11-12 . . . The strategy of hospitality shines through as Paul commands them to "Make it your ambition to lead a quiet life, to mind your own business and to work with your hands, just as we told you, so that your daily life may win the respect of outsiders and so that you will not be dependent on anybody."

> A quiet life? Mind your own business? What is Paul saying? Why

weren't the Thessalonians told to quit their jobs, give all they owned to the Apostles, and go immediately to the mission field? The answer is delightfully simple. Their first step toward building up the local church and fulfilling the Great Commission was to establish their own households as quiet places, adequately equipped, financially independent, and consistently open to outsiders.

Leading a quiet life and minding your own business are foundational to what Paul means by "winning the respect of outsiders." Hospitality, from God's point of view, is a quiet sort of thing. It fits into your normal routine. It's not always a special occasion or a disruptive activity. If there is a distinctive to biblical hospitality, this is it. It supports a quiet life. It doesn't distract the host from other responsibilities. It blends into what you have to do anyway.[3]

In the final analysis, a strong family life means a strong witness for the Lord. In the context of the local church, home education becomes a vital means for uniting families and building relations for the glory of God such that "by this shall all men know that ye are my disciples, if ye have love one to another" (John 13:35).

Relationships in the Local Church

There are two critical paths of discipleship which are lacking in most churches today—the ladies' ministry and the discipleship ministry among faithful men (2 Timothy 2:2). From the example of godly overseers (elders), young fathers can learn how to minister to their own families' needs and how to reach out to others with hospitality. The older women's ministry extends from mature women in the faith, often the elders' wives, to the younger women, teaching them how to love their husbands and children and how to reach out their hands to the poor. Before a family can reach out effectively to others in hospitality, the children must have learned to view their home as a place of ministry, as their own needs are met through their parents' loving ministry in their home.

In our day, so little ministry is directed to and through the home that the typical Christian's home life lacks significant meaning and purpose. Many have turned to home entertainment and the television to fill this vacuum. When Christian leaders try to get people involved in ministry, they often view the home (with its television and home entertainment) as competition rather than a vessel for ministry. Therefore they design "church-based programs" which pull networks of people together for outreach. Unfortunately, these programs seldom give the needy the impression that they are the recipients of true love or serious ministry nearly as much as ministry which is directed through the home can give.

In America, the changes which propelled the disappearance of home-based ministry took place about one generation apart. During the mid-1800s, fathers left their farms and home-based businesses to work in factories. More home responsibilities fell on mothers, and more children occasioned schools. Toward the end of the century, compulsory school laws required most children to attend school. This decision to move children out of the home and into schools precipitated the decline of the ministry of the older women. Because oversight for the training of children was being taken care of by the school, there was little need for the older women's ministry. Fathers and church elders became even further removed from the oversight of children's training. Within two more generations, women gained suffrage throughout the nation (1910-1920), and by 1935, Social Security opened up the way for grandparents to live independently from their children and grandchildren. Soon thereafter television moved into almost every American home, the focus of the older women's ministry moved away from the home, and ministry in and through the home was crippled.

A goal of the church-based home education ministry is to rebuild the family for ministry. When serious ministry is directed to and through the home, as it is in a home schooling ministry, television and home entertainment are set aside and people actually get excited about the fruit they are enjoying in their own hearts, the hearts of their children, and eventually the hearts of those with whom they share their exciting homes.

Communicating and Implementing

Many a good idea has met its early demise simply because there was no effective plan or means to tell others about the vision. In talking to pastors who have already established home school discipleship programs in their churches or are in the process of introducing them, I have learned that the most effective method of communicating this vision is through a discipleship program which, in principle, follows the example of our Savior. Jesus spent most of His time discipling twelve men, who in turn spread His teachings to the larger group. He developed in the twelve a servant's heart, and spent time training them in the "one-another" responsibilities which provide such a rich study for us today.

The church leadership should be united in its appreciation of how a home schooling ministry fits into the discipleship mission of the local church. If a church leader with a burden for such a discipleship ministry can introduce it on a personal basis to the other elders or leaders—one-on-one if possible—the door will be opened for the generosity of heart and sharing that is a necessary part of the ongoing ministry. Unfortunately, in some churches the leaders meet only once a month and discussion seldom goes beyond administrative concerns. Indeed, many local church leaders need to expand their own vision for ministry beyond today's standards.

The reputation of pastors as faithful ministers—not just great preachers—sets the pattern for the rest of the local church. A pastor's time is a trust which the men in the assembly must learn to value. Consequently, discipleship involves responsibility and accountability. The order of responsibility and accountability extends from obedient children to fathers, fathers to elders, and elders to the Lord Jesus Christ. The church can best minister to children by equipping the father, and assisting his helper, his wife. An overflow of love in the home will reach out to the community.

Specifics for Pastors

Pastors must carefully avoid two hazards. First, pastors must not fail to anticipate the needs of the mothers. Initially, the father's decision to home school will probably alter his wife's life more suddenly than his own. At first, while the overseers begin to work with the father to help him move toward his role as the primary teacher, the mother will need support and training. For some, this change in role is as frightening as starting a new job in a new career field. If the mothers understand that the church is committed to seeing their families through the challenges ahead, they will be less fearful or apt to stumble. If the support ministry is not clearly operating, however, some wives may seek to find ways to escape from this pressure and may even find reasons why their family ought to leave the church.

This reaction can be avoided if the ladies are assured that they will receive the support and training from veteran teachers under the ladies' ministry. Most wives are thrilled to know that the overseers of the church are committed to helping their husbands learn to take the lead in their homes. Again, this is an opportunity for the whole local church family to minister to one another.

Our local church leadership redirected the ladies' ministry to conform more closely to the ministry described in Titus 2. The ladies in our church named the new ministry "Women Growing Together." The Apostle Paul gave Titus an eight-point summary outline of the curriculum to be followed in the ladies' discipleship ministry. The older women in the faith are to teach the young women this eight-point curriculum:

1. To be sober [sensible];

2. To love their husbands;
3. To love their children;
4. To be discreet;
5. To be chaste;
6. To be keepers at home;
7. To be good; and
8. To be obedient to their own husbands.

Their work will certainly encompass studies in home schooling, craft and industry, nutrition, health, hospitality, and community outreach. I believe God will raise up experts within the local church in each of these areas if the leadership of the church is willing to give honor to these important areas of ministry.

The other hazard to avoid is the danger of allowing particular home schoolers in the congregation to be viewed as the model or standard. If this happens it can cause division. It must be clearly communicated that we all fall short of the biblical model, where the father is the primary teacher. There is as much difference between modern home schooling and biblical home schooling as there is between regular schooling and modern home schooling. Today's independent home schooler has much to learn about responsibility, submission, and ministry.

What about the men? The commitment to home school must be their personal decision. Paul tell us, "Let every man be fully persuaded in his own mind" (Romans 14:5). The church leaders should help a man be faithful to the biblical commitments he has made. A friend of mine raises sheep. Recently he explained to me that if you want sheep to go into the barn, you call the sheep, walk into the barn, and wait. They soon follow. Then you have to go out through the other side and come around behind the sheep to close the gate. He told me that if you ever call the sheep and then turn to face them, they will scatter. Sheep like to be led, but not chased. Men, too, must first indicate a desire before effective discipleship can take place.

One wise pastor I know has led three-quarters of the men in an established local church into their church-home discipleship ministry. In other words, this wise pastor had vision. He avoided the hazards mentioned above, built the barn first, put food inside, and led families safely home without chasing them.

A church's home schooling ministry must be designed to help men fulfill their biblically-mandated responsibilities: to help the father demonstrate for his family what it means to love—through his personal, self-sacrificing relationship with each family member, and for their education and edification (building up). Before a father can know what areas to focus on in his children's lives, he must know how they are measuring up to the tests they are facing daily.

Another church with a home education ministry expects fathers who have chosen to participate to sign their name under their child's name atop the tests their children take in their home education program before the child takes the test. The father's signature indicates that the father knows his child is ready to take this test (1 Corinthians 10:13). This simple requirement ensures the father's involvement. It reinforces the first link in the chain of accountability and responsibility leading from the children to the Lord Jesus Christ.

The elders of the church should not only model wise training of their own children, but should make themselves available to offer biblical instruction and encouragement to those men who are learning to embrace their God-given and wonderful responsibilities as fathers and shepherds.

I marvel at the many different ways God is leading churches into this type of ministry. Some churches start from scratch, some as an outgrowth of a Christian school. One church took their Sunday School material and trained the fathers to teach it to their families in daily devotions. This formed a bridge to help fathers realize that they can in fact teach their own children.

Endnotes

Chapter 2
Leaving Home: The Decline of the Family

1. Carle C. Zimmerman, *Family and Civilization* (New York: Harper & Brothers, 1947), p. 252.

2. Plato, *The Republic* (New York: Charles Scribner's Sons, 1928), p. 312.

3. *The World Book Encyclopedia* (Chicago: World Book Inc., 1985), vol. 16, p. 388.

4. *Ibid.*, vol. 16, p. 387.

5. *Ibid.*, vol. 16, p. 387.

6. Zimmerman, p. 387. Zimmerman quotes from *Dio Cassius Roman History* (Loeb Classical Library Edition by Earnest Cary) for the Augustan Reforms.

7. *Ibid.*, p. 401.

Chapter 3
Greek Education and the Gymnasium

1. Carle C. Zimmerman, *Family and Civilization* (New York: Harper & Brothers, 1947), p. 237.

2. William Barclay, *Educational Ideals in the Ancient World* (Philadelphia: The Westminster Press, 1959), p. 116.

3. *World Book*, vol. 8, p. 431. See also *Strong's Concordance*, number 1128, 1129, and 1131.

4. *Ibid.*, vol. 14, p. 565.

5. Barclay, p. 54.

6. Raphael Patai, *The Jewish Mind* (New York: Charles Scribner's Sons, 1977), p. 60.

Chapter 4
The Decline of Hebrew Education

1. C.B. Eavy, *History of Christian Education* (Chicago: Moody Bible Institute of Chicago, 1964), p. 50. Eavy quotes the work of a noted historian, Nathan Drazin, *History of Jewish Education from 515 B.C.E. to 220 C.E.* (Baltimore: Johns Hopkins Press, 1940), p. 11.

2. William Whiston, *Complete Works of Flavius Josephus* (Grand Rapids, Mich.: Kregel Publications, 1960), p. 609.

3. Merrill F. Unger, *Unger's Bible Dictionary* (Chicago: Moody Press, 1967), p. 1,053.

4. Nathan Drazin, *History of Jewish Education from 515 B.C.E. to 220 C.E.* (Baltimore: Johns Hopkins Press, 1940), p. 63.

5. Martin Hengel, *Judiasm and Hellinism: Studies in their Encounter in Palestine During the Early Hellenistic Period* (Philadelphia: Fortress Press, 1981), p. 73.

6. Whiston, (Josephus), p. 256.

7. Victor Tcherikover, *Hellenistic Civilization and the Jews*. Translated by S. Applebaum (New York: Atheneum Press, 1970), p. 163.

8. Whiston, (Josephus), p. 3.

9. Raphael Patai, *The Jewish Mind* (New York: Charles Scribner's Sons, 1977), p. 63.

10. Barclay, p. 38.

11. H.H. Ben Sasson, ed., *A History of the Jewish People* (Cambridge, Mass.: Harvard University Press, 1976), p. 282.

12. Chaim Potak, *Wanderings: Chaim Potak's History of the Jews* (New York: Alfred A. Knops, 1978), p. 198.

13. Whiston, (Josephus), p. 527.

14. *Ibid.*, p. 53.

Chapter 5
The Development of the American Public School

1. Robert Leight, *The First 150 Years of Education in Pennsylvania* (Harrisburg, Penn.: Pennsylvania School Board Association, 1984), p. 13.

2. Zach. Montgomery, *The School Question: From a Parental and Non-Sectarian Viewpoint* (Washington, D.C.: Gibson Brothers, 1886), p. 35.

3. Zimmerman, p. 594.

Chapter 6
Developing a Biblical Philosophy of Education

1. Merrill F. Unger, *Unger's Bible Dictionary* (Chicago: Moody Press, 1967), p. 978.

2. Glenn Doman, *How to Teach Your Baby to Read* (Philadelphia: The Better Baby Press, 1979), p. 20.

3. William Barclay, *Educational Ideals in the Ancient World* (Philadelphia: The Westminster Press, 1959), p. 16.

4. Emil Schurer, *The History of the Jewish People in the Age of Jesus Christ* (Edinburgh, Scotland: T. & T. Clark, Ltd.), p. 421.

5. Barclay, p. 17.

Chapter 7
A Helping Hand Toward Home

1.   The Institute in Basic Life Principles' excellent resource, *How to Make An Appeal*, describes ways in which great men in the Bible used situations like the one in which Daniel found himself to bring great glory to God. Also included are the experiences of those who have failed to understand the principles involved.

Chapter 8
Steps in Rebuilding

1.   Carle C. Zimmerman, *Family and Civilization* (New York: Harper & Brothers, 1947), p. 60.

2.   *Ibid.*, p. 734.

Chapter 9
A Safe Course Lies Ahead

1.   Karl Marx, *The Communist Manifesto* (Chicago: Henry Regency Company, 1969), p. 48.

2.   *Ibid.*, p. 47-48.

3.   Gregg Harris, *The Hospitality Handbook* (Gresham, Oregon: Christian Life Workshops, 1989), p. 34.

Bibliography

Adams, Blair and Joel Stein. *Salvation is of the Jews*. Austin, Texas: Truth Forum, 1988.

Albright, W.F. *The Archaeology of Palestine: A Survey of the Ancient Peoples and Cultures of the Holyland*. Rev. Ed. A volume in the Pelican Archeological Series. 1949. Reprint. Hammondsworth, Middlesex: Penguin Books, 1956.

Barclay, William. *Educational Ideals in the Ancient World*. USA: Baker, 1958.

Ben-Sasson, H.H., ed. *A History of the Jewish People*. Cambridge: Howard University Press, 1976.

Bloom, Alan. *The Closing of the American Mind*. New York: Simon and Schuster, 1987.

Doman, Glenn. *How to Teach Your Baby to Read*. Philadelphia: The Better Baby Press, 1979.

Drazin, Nathan. *History of Jewish Education from 515 B.C.E. to 220 C.E.* Baltimore: Johns Hopkins Press, 1940.

Eavey, C.B. *History of Christian Education*. Chicago: Moody Bible Institute of Chicago, 1964.

Hardenbrook, Weldon M. *Missing From Action*. Nashville: Thomas Nelson Publishers, 1987.

Hengel, Martin. *Judiasm and Hellensim: Studies in Their Encounter*

in Palestine During the Early Hellenistic Period. Translated by John
Bowden. Philadelphia: Fortress Press, 1981.

Institute in Basic Youth Conflicts, Inc. *Character Sketches, Vol. 1.*
IBLP, 1981.

Harris, Gregg. *The Hospitality Handbook.* Gresham, Oregon:
Christian Life Workshops, 1989.

Leight, Robert L. *The First 150 Years of Education in Pennsylvania.*
Harrisburg, Penn.: Pennsylvania School Board Association, 1984.

Lieberman, Saul. *Hellenism in Jewish Palestine,* vol. 18 of *Texts
and Studies of the Theological Seminary of America.* Philadelphia:
Stroock Publication Fund, 1950.

Magid, Ken and McLelvey, Carole. *High Risk: Children Without A
Conscience.* New York: Bantam Books, 1987.

Marx, Karl. *The Communist Manifesto.* Chicago: Henry Regnery
Company, 1969.

Montgomery, Zach. *The School Question from a Parental and Non-
Sectarian Viewpoint.* Washington: Gibson Bros., 1886. Reprinted by
Noah Webster Library, Robbinsdale, Minn.

Patai, Raphael. *The Jewish Mind.* New York: Charles Scribner's
Sons, 1977.

Potak, Chaim. *Wanderings: Chaim Potak's History of the Jews.*
New York: Alfred A. Knops, 1978.

Scofield, C.I., ed. *Scofield Reference Bible.* New York: Oxford
University Press, 1909.

Tcherikover, Victor. *Hellenistic Civilization and the Jews.* New
York: Atheneum, 1970.

The World Book Encyclopedia. Chicago: World Book Inc., 1985.

Unger, Merril F. *Unger's Bible Dictionary.* Chicago: Moody Press,
1967.

Whiston, William. *Complete Works of Flavius Josephus.* Grand
Rapids, Mich.: Kregel Publications, 1960.